World in the Balance

The Tauber Institute, established by a gift to Brandeis University by Dr. Laszlo N. Tauber, is dedicated to the memory of the victims of Nazi persecutions between 1933 and 1945. The Institute seeks to set into the context of modern history the causes, nature, and consequences of the crisis of European society in the second quarter of the twentieth century with a particular focus on the origins of the European Jewish catastrophe.

TAUBER INSTITUTE SERIES NO. 1

World in the Balance: Behind the Scenes of World War II
Gerhard L. Weinberg, 1981

Gerhard L. Weinberg

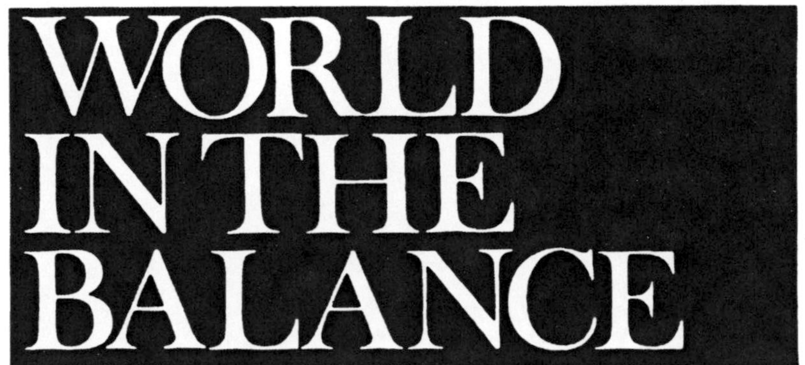

World in the Balance

Behind the Scenes of World War II

Published for Brandeis University Press by

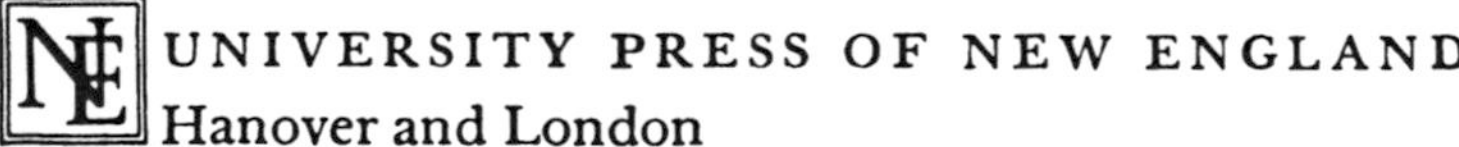

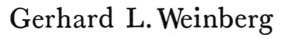

UNIVERSITY PRESS OF NEW ENGLAND
Hanover and London

University Press of New England

Brandeis University

Brown University

Clark University

Dartmouth College

University of New Hampshire

University of Rhode Island

Tufts University

University of Vermont

Library of Congress Catalogue Card Number 81-51606
International Standard Book Number 087451-216-6 (cloth)
087451-217-4 (paper)

Printed in the United States of America
Library of Congress Cataloging in Publication Data will be found on the last printed page of this book.

5 4 3

To the memory of Alistair Lloyd

Then out spake brave Horatius,
The Captain of the Gate:
"To every man upon this earth
Death cometh soon or late.
And how can man die better
Than facing fearful odds,
For the ashes of his fathers,
And the temples of his Gods."

Macaulay, *Horatius*

Contents

A map, The World in 1939, folds out of the back of the book.

Preface

The two essays which introduce this book originated as lectures prepared for delivery at Brandeis University in April 1980 under the auspices of the History Department of that university and the Martin Weiner Distinguished Lectureship Program. Their text has been revised but only to a limited extent. In a few places the phraseology has been altered for clarity or expanded slightly to include more specific illustrations for the generalizations offered. Notes have been added in order to afford the reader an opportunity to check my sources or to compare the interpretation given here with that offered by other scholars, but detailed archival references have been deliberately deferred for inclusion in a later book. The four related special studies which follow the essays have previously appeared in slightly different form; the prior location is indicated at the beginning of each. A short list of books has been appended in the bibliography which, given the immense literature on World War II, is necessarily idiosyncratic; my hope is, however, that such a list may be found useful by the reader.

I am grateful to Professors Eugene Black and Stephen Schuker of Brandeis University for arranging the two lectures. The National Endowment for the Humanities and the William Rand Kenan, Jr., Trust research fund of the University of North Carolina at Chapel Hill provided support for my research. The Imperial War Museum in London, the Public Record Office at Kew, the National Archives in Washington, the German Foreign Ministry Archive in Bonn, the German Federal Archives in Koblenz, the German Military Archive in Freiburg, and the Institute for Contemporary History in Munich were all helpful to a demanding visitor in search of material for this work.

Through the generosity of Mr. and Mrs. A. C. B. Lloyd, I was able to spend the first year of World War II as a student in their school in Swanage, Dorset, England. That was a time when memorization was still believed to be a significant element in the education of the young, and Macaulay's "Horatius" was on the program. The Lloyds' only son, an officer in the Royal Artillery, was mortally wounded on D-Day; it is to his memory that this work is dedicated.

Chapel Hill, North Carolina
November 1980

Introduction

The purpose of this book is to suggest a way in which the dramatic events of World War II may be seen. My work on the history of that conflict is far from complete; and while I have tried to take into account much of the literature as well as information from such newly opened records as the American Magic and the British Ultra intercepts of Japanese, German, and Italian messages, it is very likely that further research, new information, and differing interpretations will lead to changes in my own views. There are, however, two facets of the war that already appear to me not seriously subject to challenge, and both are central to the tentative summary here presented. In the first place, I am convinced that the war must be seen as a whole, and that the presentation of it in discrete segments covering the European and Pacific portions separately distorts reality and obscures important aspects of the war on both sides of the world. The Sino-Japanese War which began in July 1937, however terrible for the participants, would have remained a localized war in East Asia like the Sino-Japanese War of 1894-95 or the Russo-Japanese War of 1904-5 had not the initiative of Germany in Europe opened up, for some in the Japanese government, the appearance of an opportunity for vast additional conquests.

Neither the transformation of the Sino-Japanese war into a portion of the wider conflict nor the subsequent development of the Pacific War can be understood without reference to the course of war in Europe. Similarly, events in the Pacific came to have crucial implications for the European theater. However much we may need to concentrate at some point in any narrative on one area, therefore, the events in that area must always be seen as part of a larger world-wide whole.

A second prerequisite for any understanding of the great struggle is a mental self-liberation from the certain knowledge of its outcome. In desperate struggles millions fought and died, hopeful or fearful—or both—but without our awareness of the end. And uncertainty about the future course of hostilities was as characteristic of leaders as of ordinary people. There were hopes—often dashed; expectations—sometimes disappointed; and fears—frequently realized; but even the most careful preparations rarely produced certain results. Some were more and some less accurate in their estimates of the future, but all moved uneasily through the fog of war. Any account which ignores the uncertainties inherent in developments, overlooks the role of chance, assumes as foregone the results of battles, or minimizes the impact of the unanticipated is sure to distort reality. Troops and supplies can occasionally be moved on railroad tracks along lines clearly marked on maps and at intervals geared to a time schedule. But war generally brings the unexpected, and often with dramatic suddenness.

While the two essays provide a general preview of a new look at World War II, the four studies which follow examine in greater detail some critical aspects of that conflict. They are all focused on Germany and to a considerable extent on Hitler because the configuration of the whole war depended so largely on initiatives taken in Berlin. One approach that appears to me to be essential for any examination of the war is to try to see it through the eyes of key participants. The review of "Hitler's Image of the United States" traces the broad outlines of the German leader's view of America from the 1920's to his last days in the Berlin bunker. We can see here how ideological preconceptions affected the policy of Germany in peace and her strategy in war.

The demarcation between peace and war came for the United States in December 1941. The open junction of the European and East Asian conflicts into one world-wide conflagration took place forty years ago; Germany's part in that junction is examined in the second piece. The question asked anxiously in Washington in late 1941—and occasionally speculated upon in the years since 1945—was, what would happen if Japan struck in East Asia but Germany did not move against the United States? How could the contingency planning of the United States and Great Britain which postulated a "Europe First" strategy for any joint war possibly be implemented if the United States were involved only in the Pacific? As this book shows, the anxiety was unnecessary then and the speculations are foolish now: it was just the other way around. Without the prior urging and assurances from Berlin, those pushing for war in Tokyo would never had had their way: it was Berlin that might have moved entirely on its own.

Germany might have gone to war with the United States without an ally in the Pacific, and was indeed making some provisions for that contingency, but Japan at no time seriously considered fighting the United States and Great Britain by herself. Hitler and Hermann Göring, the head of Germany's air force, were authorizing the development of bombers to strike at New York and other East Coast cities as early as 1937; and if nothing much eventually came of these projects, it was not for lack of trying.[1] The Japanese, on the other hand, had not accepted the plan for an attack on Pearl Harbor until October 1941,[2] even

1. This whole subject is in need of detailed examination. By far the best review of it currently available is in Jochen Thies, *Architekt der Weltherrschaft: Die "Endziele" Hitlers* (Düsseldorf: Droste, 1976), pp. 136-48.

2. A useful summary is in Robert E. Ward, "The Inside Story of the Pearl Harbor Plan," *United States Naval Institute Proceedings*, 77, No. 12 (Dec. 1951), pp. 1171-83.

though their decision to strike South had been taken a few months earlier. In this broader context, we can now see that Japan indeed took the initiative on her own on December 7, 1941, but only within a wider war already started by Germany and while being strongly urged forward by the latter.[3] And the naval plans of the Germans, as well as their air force expectations, in any case looked to war against the United States as a portion of broader world-wide ambitions. Because those ambitions were cut short by defeat in war, their dimensions are not always perceived clearly; but the intended trajectory of Germany's ascent must be kept in mind if decisions made along the way are to be understood. It is in this context that the colonial projects of the Third Reich come into the picture.

One dramatic way in which World War II changed the world was by its acceleration of the process of decolonization. World War I furthered the emergence of the British Dominions as independent states on the international scene, led to the launching of new experiments at self-government in India, and undermined the whole system of European colonial rule; and it was the collapse of colonial structures in World War II that opened the way for a recasting of Africa, Asia, and the Near East in the years after 1945. Hitler's war had been intended to lead to the creation of a vast world empire ruled from correspondingly stupendous buildings in Berlin.[4] Instead, it led to the consolidation of a Soviet Empire in Central and East Europe as well as the maintenance of Russian control over the Central and East Asian areas acquired by the Romanovs, while all the other colonial empires dissolved into independent states.

Before World War II, the British and French had tried to restrain Germany from aggression in Central and East

3. We must accordingly somewhat shift the accents given to this issue by Hans L. Trefousse, "Germany and Pearl Harbor," *Far Eastern Quarterly,* 11 (Nov. 1951), pp. 35-50.

4. Thies, chaps. 1 and 2.

Europe by offering her African colonies and economic concessions, but the German government had invariably rejected all such approaches precisely because all the proposed concessions were tied to keeping Germany from the conquests in the East which were the primary focus of her ambitions.[5] But unwillingness to pay the price of restraint in Europe for a return to the scramble for African empire did not mean lack of interest in such an empire. Germany would take what she wanted in Africa as in Eastern Europe—she would, in Hitler's terms, be a world empire or nothing.[6]

The way in which the first stages of Germany's intended re-entry into the colonial field had been visualized at the time is described by the article on "German Colonial Plans and Policies, 1938-1942." Although there has been further work on the subject in the almost two decades since this piece was written,[7] the broad outlines presented in it remain unchallenged. It can, therefore, serve to illustrate the way in which colonial empire fitted into the broader concerns of the Third Reich and the interaction between that project and other policies in the years of Germany's rapid ascent to a world role and of her slipping from that pinnacle.

In the eyes of some readers these articles, like the two essays, may appear to give disproportionate attention to the person of Adolf Hitler, to his views, choices, and decisions, with relatively less emphasis being placed on broader

5. These projects, and the German rejection of them, are reviewed in detail in Gerhard L. Weinberg, *The Foreign Policy of Hitler's Germany: Starting World War II, 1937-1939* (Chicago: University of Chicago Press, 1980), chaps. 3 and 4.

6. Originally analyzed by Günter Moltmann, "Weltherrschaftsideen Hitlers," in Otto Brunner and Dietrich Gerhard (eds.), *Europa und Übersee, Festschrift für Egmont Zechlin* (Hamburg: Hans Bredow-Institut, 1961), pp. 197-240, this aspect of Hitler's thinking is now covered in detail in the book by Thies.

7. In particular, the big book by Klaus Hildebrand, *Vom Reich zum Weltreich: Hitler, NSDAP und koloniale Frage, 1919-1945* (Munich: Fink, 1969).

trends, forces, and developments in German and world society. What is too frequently ignored, however, is that if once vast masses in a country have concluded that their present and future welfare is best entrusted to the preferences of one person, then those preferences assume critical importance, especially if the society holding such views is an advanced and powerful one. Having unconditionally surrendered their will to Hitler, vast numbers of Germans thereby reinforced his importance by their dedicated support, regardless of the differences some of them might have had with his views in matters of detail. Only opposition on fundamental grounds could produce a real challenge, and those few who were so inclined quickly recognized the same centrality of Hitler's role. The internal opponents of Hitler concentrated on removing him from the scene because they could see that a new arrangement of German institutions and policies could take place only after his arrest or assassination. He could not make war without both a mass following in the country and the subservience of its elite, but that war could not be ended unless Hitler had first been removed.

The text of the talk I gave to commemorate the twenty-fifth anniversary of the attempt to kill Hitler on July 20, 1944, surveys the problems faced by those who tried to change the ruinous course of events. Since the effort failed, we will never know how success would have altered subsequent developments, but it should be obvious that an end of the war in Europe in 1943 or 1944—to say nothing of 1939—would have produced a world very different from that which emerged as a result of Germany's fighting on to the bitter end.

It may offend the susceptibilities of many to be told that any figure of such miserable personal qualities as a Hitler could exert such great influence on the lives—and deaths—of the inhabitants of our planet. The very discrepancy between the mean and vindictive man with a mind cluttered by preposterous inanities on the one hand, and the almost incomprehensible dimensions of a global conflict on the other, is an affront to one's sense of proportion. It should, however, remind us all the more forcefully of the great dangers when the decisions over peace and war are made by persons not subject to restraint in an age of weapons of mass destruction. It is a dim hope, but an important one all the same, that the memory of the great calamity and its horrifying human and material costs will add to whatever restraints there may be.

World in the Balance

World War II: The Axis, 1939-1942

If, instead of dealing with the Second World War, I were now to discuss the Second Silesian War or the Second Burmese War, keeping the number but shifting to the eighteenth or nineteenth century, readers might be surprised, even disappointed, but there would be two advantages. In the first place, I could be reasonably confident that most readers would look at the second essay, if only to find out how that war came out. In the second place, and closely related to the implications of what has just been said, few would consider what they read through a framework of preconceptions.

The Second World War has come to impress itself on people's memories in a variety of ways; and these memories have been molded and distorted to such an extent that, whatever effect those memories themselves have on later events, the war is obscured as often as it is illuminated by them. We see the relatively recent past through the events lying between it and the present, rather than through the events *preceding* the focus of our attention, and thereby we often do violence to reality. Just as the public and political figures saw and participated in the 1980 campaign in terms of their perception of that and *prior* campaigns and events, not from a knowledge of events between 1980 and 2000, so the development of World War II should be looked at with reference to the world as seen by contemporaries and their understanding of the decades that preceded it.

It is not my intention to suggest that we not ask new questions of the past or that we ignore events since 1945. I do argue, however, that we are more likely to misconstrue than to illuminate the past if we disregard the reality that sequence is always in chronological order. Only the dimmest glimmerings of possible future developments accompany the assumptions about the past, concerns of the present, and hopes and fears about coming events in the minds of those making choices and decisions on the historical scene.

As we approach the great catastrophe of World War II, any effort at comprehension is both aided and hampered by the overwhelming mass of published and unpublished material available to the scholar. Books have appeared and continue to appear in an unending stream.[1] American, German, British, and Italian archives are to a large extent open to research. Beyond this, there are further mountains of evidence only now in the process of being opened up—the cryptographic material, to mention only one prominent example[2]—while still other huge piles were either destroyed

1. A small sampling of the literature is given in the Bibliography below.

2. The British government allowed release of information on British code-breaking beginning in 1974, and a steadily increasing body of declassified records made available at the Public Record Office has inspired much discussion. The first volume of the British official history of this and related efforts, Francis H. Hinsley, et al., *British Intelligence in the Second World War: Its Influence on Strategy and Operations* (New York: Cambridge University Press, 1979), is useful but leaves much to be desired. A very fine survey is that of Ronald Lewin, *Ultra Goes to War* (New York: McGraw-Hill, 1978). The papers and discussion at a conference in November 1978 of participants and historians about the role of signals intelligence in World War II has been published by Jürgen Rohwer and Eberhard Jäckel (eds.), *Die Funkaufklärung und ihre Rolle im Zweiten Weltkrieg* (Stuttgart: Motorbuch, 1979); an English language edition is to be published by the Naval Institute Press.

Some American cryptographic material from World War II was originally released during the Pearl Harbor hearings in 1945-46 (see Gerhard L. Weinberg's introduction to the reprint of the congressional hearings, documents, and report, *Pearl Harbor Attack* [New York: AMS, 1973]). A major program for declassifying additional documents was inaugurated by the National Security Agency, the present custodian of such records, in 1977, and has resulted in the transfer of important materials to the National Archives.

German cryptographic records captured by the Western Powers in World War II are held in England under joint British-American control. As a result of a ruling by the Interagency Classification Review Committee,

in the war[3] or remain, and are likely to continue, closed to view.[4] These two essays suggest a path through this thicket by a historian attempting to look at it afresh after spending many years on the war's origins.[5]

War had been an intended and even a preferred part of National Socialist policy from the beginning, not primarily out of a preference for fighting for its own sake, but from an entirely accurate conviction that the aim of German expansion could be secured only by war. Germany was to seize the agricultural land needed to feed her population, a population that would grow further as it obtained such land, and which would accordingly expand its needs and its lands into the indefinite future. This crude Social Darwinism, in which racial groups fought for the land which could provide the means of subsistence, expelling or exterminating but never assimilating other groups, was derived from a view of history as deterministic as that of Marx, but substituting race for class as the key to understanding.[6] Its application had internal as well as external implications. The Jews were seen as the most immediate

the National Security Agency was obliged to open some of these records in 1977-78, but the agency decided in 1980 that the rest should be closed for "the foreseeable future" and that the documents should henceforth be treated as having been handed over in confidence to the United States by the Hitler government.

3. Some destruction was deliberate as one side or the other destroyed records to keep them from falling into the hands of its enemies; an example would be the Germans' massive destruction of the bulk of their own air force records. Other records were destroyed as a result of military operations. Perhaps the most notable example of this was the loss of the bulk of the German army archive in Potsdam in an air raid in April 1945.

4. The Soviet archives are closed to scholars. Those of Italy and Japan are partially open. The French may be opened in ten years.

5. Gerhard L. Weinberg, *The Foreign Policy of Hitler's Germany: Diplomatic Revolution in Europe, 1933-1936* and *Starting World War II, 1937-1939* (Chicago: University of Chicago Press, 1970, 1980).

6. Weinberg, *Foreign Policy 1933-1936,* chap. 1, provides a brief summary with evidence from the pre-1933 period.

threat to racial purity inside Germany, and as the main motor of resistance outside the country. A policy of extreme anti-Semitism would accordingly be a central concern of the government in peace first and in war later. Furthermore, a key internal need was the urgency of increasing the birthrate of the allegedly better and reducing the birthrate of the supposedly inferior racial stocks in the population, measures that required a dictatorial regime which alone could in addition prepare the way for, and hope to succeed in, the wars a racial policy called for in external affairs. Measured by the criterion of feeding a growing German population with the products of its own agricultural land, the boundaries Germany had once had were almost as useless as those of the 1920's; and thus a revision of the Versailles Peace Treaty of 1919 could be only a propaganda excuse and never a goal of German policy. The vast reaches to be obtained would never be granted peacefully, and war was therefore both necessary and inevitable.

But war the last time had meant disaster for Germany. As those in charge in Germany in the 1930's saw it, disaster had been the result of the collapse of the home front, produced by a combination of false promises from abroad and traitors at home under the strain of years of almost deadlocked fighting against a host of enemies.[7] The dictatorship at home would preclude any role for traitors; a careful attention to new methods of warfare would prevent deadlock; a sequence of separate wars would obviate having to fight a hostile coalition; and the successes of a series of short wars—*Blitzkriege* or lightning wars—would make it possible to avoid imposing great hardships on the homefront. It would all be done right the next time. Casualties would be incurred, but the absence of deadlock would re-

7. The importance of this consideration for German policy has been stressed by the works of Timothy W. Mason. See, for example, his *Sozialpolitik im Dritten Reich: Arbeiterklasse und Volksgemeinschaft,* 2d ed. (Opladen: Westdeutscher Verlag, 1978).

duce their number, and the conquest of new living space would lead to the rapid replacement of losses by the higher birthrate of the pioneer farmers settled in place of the dispossessed.

The bulk of the land to be conquered was in Russia, which, by what Hitler considered a stroke of particularly good fortune for Germany, had been taken over by what he believed to be a group of Jewish Bolsheviks who were incapable of organizing the—in any case inferior—largely Slavic population for effective resistance. The real obstacles lay elsewhere. Germany was in the middle of Europe and would have to establish a completely secure position there before heading East. France was the closest main enemy and Czechoslovakia the closest minor one. The sequence of wars would therefore be Czechoslovakia first, France second, then the drive East, and thereafter elsewhere. In the decade 1924-34 Hitler had thought that war with England could be postponed until after Russia, but events early in his rule had disabused him of this illusion, and by 1935 he was convinced of the opposite. The way in which the British, as he believed, had tricked and bluffed him out of war in the crisis over Czechoslovakia in 1938 confirmed him in his determination to settle with both Western Powers as soon as possible. The winter of 1938-39 was accordingly devoted to the military and diplomatic preparations for that project.

The key German diplomatic preparations succeeded only in part. Since Poland would not accept satellite status and thus enable Hitler to crush the West without danger in the East, that country would be the victim of his first war, with the West to follow thereafter. His outrage over having been cheated out of war in 1938 made him all the more determined to have it in 1939. This insistence on war was reinforced by his view that others might catch up with and even overtake Germany's headstart in armaments, as well as by his own preference for fighting at a relatively youthful age, fearful of short life for himself and a lack of equal resolution in any successor.[8]

The Poles preferred peace with their powerful German and Russian neighbors but would not subordinate themselves to either; they would fight rather than surrender their newly restored independence. Great Britain and France alone of the world's powers were willing to go to war with Germany although not yet attacked themselves. What about the other nations?

Italy had ambitions of her own, but the efforts to obtain some of them in East Africa and Spain had so strained her limited resources that, although tied to Germany by an offensive and defensive alliance since May 1939, she felt unable to enter a major war as yet. She would help only from the sidelines. Japan was pursuing her ambitions in China, had as a result blundered ever deeper into hostilities on the mainland, and would have been happy for an alliance with Germany—but *not* against England and France, behind whom she saw the United States. What Japan wanted was an alliance against the Soviet Union with which she had many differences and on whose East Asian territories Tokyo had long looked with covetous eyes. Any alliance of this type was, however, out of phase with Germany's desire for an alliance against the West. On the contrary, at the very time that the Japanese thought of mediating between Germany and Poland in order to maintain what they saw as a barrier to Soviet expansion in Europe, the Germans were responding to the sorts of approaches from Stalin that in prior years they had regularly waved aside. From the standpoint of Berlin, moreover, the hesitations of Tokyo made the friendly signals from Moscow all the more interesting.

While Japan had needed no encouragement from Rus-

8. The crisis over Czechoslovakia and German policy thereafter leading to the outbreak of war are covered in Weinberg, *Foreign Policy 1937-1939*, chaps. 10-14.

sia to embroil herself in war in China, the Germans had funked at war in 1938 and might do so again. In Stalin's view, therefore, knowing that Germany planned to turn West after crushing Poland, a Soviet policy which gave the Germans some encouragement could assist them in taking the plunge into war this time. Germany might pay and pay heavily for assistance from the Soviet Union in a war from which Russia could abstain to the damage of others and to her own profit. Stalin explained this view about as frankly as he could to British Ambassador Sir Stafford Cripps in July 1940, pointing out that "the U.S.S.R. had wanted to change the old equilibrium . . . but that England and France had wanted to preserve it. Germany had also wanted to make a change in the equilibrium, and this common desire to get rid of the old equilibrium had created the basis for the rapprochement with Germany."[9] British Prime Minister Neville Chamberlain and French Prime Minister Edouard Daladier believed that Germany with her great strength and headstart in armaments could be held in check or defeated only by a war on several fronts; President Roosevelt, who was dubious about the power of France, tried to convince Stalin that this was a correct view, but the Soviet leader would not make this discovery until June of 1941.

Germany could thus start the war if she so wanted—and her government wanted to very much indeed—under circumstances in which only Poland, Britain, and France were

9. The report of Cripps of July 16, 1940 is in the Public Record Office, FO 371/24846, f. 10, N 6526/30/38; it is quoted with the permission of the Controller of Her Majesty's Stationery Office.

Internally the Soviet government was more direct. An instruction of the Soviet Commissariat for Foreign Affairs of July 1, 1940, to the Ambassador in Tokyo contains the sentence: "The conclusion of our agreement with Germany was dictated by the need for a war in Europe." The full text of this document is in James W. Morley (ed.), *The Fateful Choice: Japan's Road to the Pacific War* (New York: Columbia University Press, 1980), pp. 311-12. Neither of the documents quoted was available to me when I wrote *Foreign Policy 1937-1939*, but they confirm the interpretation of Soviet foreign policy offered there.

against her, with the Soviet Union assisting, Italy cheering, Japan temporarily stupefied, and the remaining powers in a range of positions more or less favorable to one side or the other. While Italy's Mussolini looked forward to joining at an opportune moment and the Spanish dictator Francisco Franco at times entertained similar thoughts, the Japanese would rethink their approach. The other neutrals tried to devise ways to stay out of the new conflict, ranging from the Soviet Union's idea of helping Hitler on an increasing scale to the American scheme of helping Hitler's enemies, also on an increasing scale. The initiative, however, lay with Germany, who naturally preferred to have the neutrals help her, but made her own decisions largely without reference to such considerations.

The crushing German attack on Poland in the face of the defensive posture of France enabled Hitler to return in practice to his concept of striking in the West with all his forces because of a quiet situation in the East, while at the same time the alignment with Russia largely eliminated any serious impact from the Allied blockade. The Soviet Union not only provided extensive supplies of raw materials critical to the German war economy, but also assisted German acquisition of such materials from third countries by facilitating their transit across Soviet territory.[10] At the urging of his naval advisers, who wanted oceanic bases, and to make sure that there would be no interference with the iron supplies from Sweden which were essential for Germany's armaments industry, Hitler attacked Norway and Denmark in April 1940. Germany's success in this operation came at the cost of heavy losses to the German navy, losses which would have major implications for any German hope of invading England that year,[11]

10. There is a preliminary survey of this subject in Gerhard L. Weinberg, *Germany and the Soviet Union, 1939-1941* (Leyden: Brill, 1954, 1972), pp. 65-75. The effort of the British to close this gap in the blockade is summarized in William N. Medlicott, *The Economic Blockade*, 1 (London: H.M. Stationery Office, 1952), pp. 312-28, 633-63, 667-72.

11. The term "losses" in this context includes not only the many ships

but it did open up vistas to the oceans from Norwegian bases.

After repeated postponements caused by weather and internal objections, the major offensive in the West came in May 1940. For the only time in World War II Germany could concentrate all her land, sea, and air forces in one theater on one project. Designed to defeat France and enable Germany to crush England with the seizure of air bases in the Low Countries and naval bases on the French Atlantic coast, the operation had been visualized along these general lines by Hitler at least since May of 1939.[12] It was now carried out with breathtaking speed. The neutral Low Countries were overrun as a suitable reward for their prior shielding of Germany's industrial heart, the French routed, and the British run off the continent to Germany's great happiness, Russian applause, and Italian—and for a while even Spanish—eagerness to participate in the spoils.

For a moment it looked as if a new world were at hand. This war seemed to be over, even if the thick-headed British might take a few weeks to figure that out. Postwar planning went forward rapidly in the German government during June and July 1940. There were schemes for redrawing the map of Western Europe.[13] There were the projects for organizing and administering the new German colonial empire in Africa.[14] And the racial reorganization of Europe might be assisted by the latter process. Hitler

---

sunk but also those damaged, like the *Gneisenau* and *Scharnhorst,* and therefore laid up for repairs during the critical weeks in the summer when they would have been needed to protect an invasion.

12. The general outline of this strategy is in Hitler's speech to high German military leaders on May 23, 1939, printed in *Akten zur deutschen auswärtigen Politik 1918-1945,* Series D, Vol. 6 (Baden-Baden: Imprimerie Nationale, 1956), No. 433. Hitler's address to his generals on May 28, 1938, had already suggested essentially the same strategy (Weinberg, *Foreign Policy 1937-1939,* p. 371).

13. Eberhard Jäckel, *Frankreich in Hitlers Europa* (Stuttgart: Deutsche Verlags-Anstalt, 1966), pp. 46-54.

14. There is a summary in my article on "German Colonial Plans and Policies, 1938-1942," reprinted here on pp. 96-136.

had already ordered a massive program of murdering allegedly defective German babies, the mentally ill, and the sick and elderly people believed unproductive in October 1939, and tens of thousands were being slaughtered accordingly. The defeat of France now opened up the possibility of dealing with another portion of the racial problem: the Jews of Europe could be deported to Madagascar. The island in the Indian Ocean then under French control might provide a suitably distant and isolated location to which the Jews of German-dominated Europe might be sent.[15]

As for the future military operations of the Third Reich, these would require larger air and naval forces, so the army could now be reduced with emphasis shifted to the other services. In particular, the big program for the construction of a fleet of battleships and aircraft carriers, temporarily shelved in September 1939, could be reactivated, while the German government secured bases on and off the northwest coast of Africa for their employment. All available evidence suggests that in the great naval construction program for the years *after* the defeat of England and France, Hitler and his advisers were looking across the Atlantic toward the United States as the next enemy.[16]

All these fine prospects ran into difficulties in the summer of 1940. The British government had refused to consider peace in the winter of 1939-40 unless the independence of Czechoslovakia and Poland were first restored.[17]

15. A survey of the history of the "Madagascar Plan" is in Christopher Browning, *The Final Solution and the German Foreign Office: A Study of Referat D III of Abteilung Deutschland, 1940-43* (New York: Holmes & Meier, 1978), pp. 35-43.

16. This issue is discussed in more detail on pp. 81-85.

17. The account of these soundings in Bernd Martin, *Friedensinitiativen und Machtpolitik im Zweiten Weltkrieg, 1939-1942* (Düsseldorf; Droste, 1974), chaps. 1-3, misconstrues the evidence available at the Public Record Office. Those records clearly show that both the French and British governments realized that only a fundamental reversal of the German policy of depriving neighboring countries of their independence offered any hope of safety for Britain and France. Although not entirely in agreement on the postwar future of Austria, the British and French believed it obvious that both the Czechs and the Poles would have to have their independence

Now it was determined to hold on. In secret the British shipped their gold and foreign exchange assets to Canada;[18] in public they rallied to Churchill's defiant voice. In the air they held the German air force, and at sea they challenged the Germans to try crossing the Channel. As the London government looked to a grim future, it faced three critical questions beyond the immediate one of survival: could the sea lanes be kept open, could military supplies be obtained from the United States although British funds would run out,[19] and how could Germany possibly be defeated? The answer to the first would lie in endless battle above, on, and under the ocean, and to the second in American policy changes. The only feasible answer to the third question appeared to be to strike back at Germany in the air; victorious on land and halted at sea, Germany might be brought low enough by destruction from above so that the structure she was creating in Europe would collapse. The fighter planes of the Royal Air Force were Britain's key hope for defense in 1940, but her bombers would carry the war back to the country that had started it all. Those who had set the world on fire would yet see their own roofs aflame.

In the summer of 1940 Hitler determined that if Britain would not surrender willingly, she must be blasted into it

---

restored to them as part of any peace settlement. Neither was willing to contemplate peace without such provision—and the German government was unwilling to consider peace with it.

18. The implications of these shipments of about five billion dollars worth of gold and securities ordered in mid-June 1940 and begun later that month have not been properly integrated into existing studies of the war. There is a popular account, based primarily on interviews, by Leland Stowe, "The Secret Voyage of Britain's Treasure," *Reader's Digest,* 34, Nov. 1955, pp. 17-26.

19. Note the reference to this issue in the first letter Churchill wrote as Prime Minister to President Roosevelt on May 15, 1940: "We shall go on paying dollars for as long as we can, but I should like to feel reasonably sure that when we can pay no more, you will give the stuff all the same." Francis L. Loewenheim, et al. (eds.), *Roosevelt and Churchill: Their Secret Wartime Correspondence* (New York: Saturday Review Press/E. P. Dutton, 1975), p. 95.

by bombing or beaten into it by invasion. But the implementation of this design proved very difficult as resistance to the former foretold that probable disaster awaited the latter. Perhaps the indirect approach was both simpler and safer. An attack on the Soviet Union would be required in any case in order to seize the agricultural space Germany needed; was not this a good time for that operation? After the spectacular victory over France, such an expedition certainly looked a lot easier than an invasion of England, and it would also assist with the defeat of England by removing her remaining hopes of outside assistance. A crushed Soviet state could never offer assistance to Britain herself, while the liberation of Japan from danger at her backdoor would enable that power to move south against Britain in East Asia, immobilize the United States in the Pacific, and thereby deprive England of hope for aid from that quarter as well. A shift to land war in the East would, it was true, again mean deferring the great naval program in favor of a renewed buildup of the army, but this disadvantage would last only a short time. The Americans, ineffectual except as braggarts, would be kept in check by Japan's advance until Germany could return to her naval program.[20]

What conclusions were drawn by others from Germany's stunning triumph in Western Europe? The Americans were awakened rather rudely from two decades of slumber. Civilians are often so amused by what they see as the attempts of military leaders to win the last war, that they fail to recognize the at least equivalent foolishness of their own efforts to stay out of it. Just as wars once over cannot be refought, so wars in which one has once been involved cannot be avoided. Such conceptual impossibilities have rarely inhibited anyone, and Americans who thought entrance into World War I had been a mistake were as single-mindedly determined to stay out of it in the 1930's as they are

20. This matter is covered in more detail on pp. 83-86.

to keep out of Vietnam today. The sudden realization in 1940 that what they confronted was *not* the real or imagined challenge of the Kaiser but an entirely different danger produced a series of dramatic new policy departures, most of them bitterly debated in a country disoriented by the very suddenness of developments.

The shocked recognition that a country facing two oceans might no longer be able to depend on Britain to ward off possible dangers in one of these, would lead to plans for the construction of a "two-ocean navy" as eventual successor to a fleet which might be switched back and forth through the Panama Canal but could not defend the country in both oceans at the same time. On land, Americans had seen Belgium overrun in less than three weeks—but Belgium had put into the field in May 1940 an army of eighteen divisions, more than three times as many as the five-division force that the United States could have sent into battle that month![21] Under these circumstances, increasing numbers of Americans began to support a serious effort to build up a military force of substantial rather than infinitesimal proportions, though like the naval program, that project would take a lot of time to implement in practice. Alarmed but not as surprised as some by the German advance, Franklin Roosevelt decided to break with tradition and to seek a third term—and the electorate would reveal the extent of its alarm by granting it.[22] The steps toward new policies of American rearmament and

21. For Belgium's army, there is a fair summary in Brian Bond, *France and Belgium, 1939-1940* (London: Davis-Poynter, 1975); for the American army, see the summary in Robert Dallek, *Franklin D. Roosevelt and American Foreign Policy, 1932-1945* (New York: Oxford University Press, 1979), p. 221.

22. The views of Roosevelt on the relationship between the German threat and the power of France have not been investigated sufficiently. His very personal handling of diplomacy included careful attention to the reports of his handpicked ambassadors to France, Jesse I. Strauss and William C. Bullitt, both of whom regularly stressed the weakness of France. Could it be that the president's naval proclivities made him less susceptible to the aura surrounding the French army after World War I? For his attempts to assist the build-up of the French air force, see John M. Haight,

aid to Britain were accompanied by endless controversy, but the signs of awakening were indeed discernible. The resistance of others would enable the United States eventually to play a major role herself.

The Soviet Union may have been surprised at the speed of Germany's victory in the West, but after quickly taking over the remaining loot Hitler had promised the previous year—just in case peace did break out—Stalin believed he could sit back and wait. Unresponsive to British and later to American attempts to awaken him to the dangers ahead, he preferred to adhere to his earlier policy of avoiding war by assistance to Germany. Ideological preconceptions blinded Hitler to the potential power of both the Soviet Union and the United States, and similarly obscured from the Soviet leader's vision the reality of German devotion to the desire for agricultural land. If National Socialism was seen—and sometimes still is seen—as simply an agency of monopoly capitalism, its racial ideology must be window-dressing to ensnare the masses and of no significance for policy. Self-delusion on this score had led the German Communists to view the German Socialists rather than the Nazis as the main danger in the 1920's and early 1930's; it remains observable today in the dispute over a memorial to the tens of thousands of Jews from Kiev murdered at Babi Yar and the absence of a monument to Jews among the many memorials at Auschwitz.

Whatever does not fit the theory cannot be, and the Soviet leaders could no more accept at the time than before or subsequently the reality of an ideology of racial agrarian expansionism. In 1927 when there were no signs of military preparations anywhere for an attack on the Soviet Union, there had been a major war scare in Russia because ideological constraints suggested a danger where

---

Jr., *American Aid to France, 1938-1940* (New York: Atheneum, 1970); for his 1939 effort to persuade Stalin to align himself with Britain and France because a German victory in the West would endanger the Soviet Union as well as the United States, see my *Foreign Policy 1937-1939*, pp. 578, 608.

none existed; now the situation was reversed, with plenty of signs but an iron determination to misconstrue them. From Moscow's perspective, the Germans with their great victories over the other imperialists in the West now had access to all the markets they could want, the opportunity to seize all the colonies their greedy hearts might desire, and, with Soviet willingness to supply whatever their own empire might still lack, no objective reason to head East. It is too often forgotten that the Soviet Union was prepared in the winter of 1940-41 to join with the powers of the Tripartite Pact, Germany, Italy, and Japan, in the war against England.[23] The Germans refused to discuss the terms of adhesion because months before they had decided to invade the Soviet Union. Berlin preferred receiving supplies from Russia until a few minutes before the attack over engaging in lengthy and detailed negotiations that could only cause problems in regard to the very deliveries Germany needed from Russia for the forthcoming march East.

Japan saw opening before her eyes the glorious prospect of conquests in South and Southeast Asia as one by one the colonial masters of the lands rich in oil, tin, and rubber fell before the German onslaught. Was not this the time to strike? A working agreement might be reached with Russia, but what about the United States? Guam could be ignored, but hardly the Philippines. The Americans had already decided to leave the Philippines in 1946, and it is surely no coincidence that to the insistent German urging that they attack in the South, the Japanese repeatedly mentioned that year as the one in which they would be

23. The Soviet offer of November 25, 1940, to adhere to the Tripartite Pact has not been appropriately assimilated into accounts of the war. It must be placed in context with the simultaneous and eventually successful negotiations with Germany over the cession of Germany's claim to a portion of Lithuania, the refusal of the Soviet Union to respond favorably to approaches from London, and the disregard by the Soviet Union of the first concrete warnings from the United States of German plans for the attack on Russia.

ready to move. But the leaders in Tokyo knew well enough that by *that* time, the war Germany had started might well be over, and that if they wanted to take advantage of the situation, this was indeed, as Berlin maintained, the right time to act. Long internal debates over the issue proceeded in Tokyo;[24] the beginnings of American rearmament worried them; and even the German promise to join in war against the United States if Japan became embroiled in war with that country did not resolve all doubts. As the Germans had not informed them of their decision to attack Russia, the Japanese worried about their rear if they moved South, and only after the German invasion of June 1941 did they decide to plunge forward.[25]

The Italian and Spanish dictators both wanted to join in Hitler's victorious war—after the fighting but before the division of the loot. Mussolini jumped in without either asking for assurances as to his share of the spoils or making any serious preparations for real fighting. This led to a string of disasters: the Germans could not deliver the spoils Mussolini wanted lest large parts of the French empire come back into the war on England's side, and the armed forces of Italy were entirely unprepared for the conflict into which their leader had flung them.[26] The struggle for East Africa and the Mediterranean was lost by Italy by the spring of 1941—with several hundred thousand Italian soldiers killed or captured in the process—and only the intervention of Germany kept the Mediterranean theater active for an additional two years.

Franco had been more cautious. He sent his list of de-

24. On this subject, see the book edited by James Morley cited in n. 9, above. For the subsequent period, see Nobutake Ike (ed.), *Japan's Decision for War: Records of the 1941 Policy Conferences* (Stanford, Calif.: Stanford University Press, 1967).

25. See also the discussion herein on pp. 85-91.

26. A useful summary in John Whittam, "The Italian General Staff and the Coming of the Second World War," in Adrian Preston (ed.), *General Staffs and Diplomacy before the Second World War* (London: Croom Helm, 1978), pp. 77-97

mands to Berlin on June 19, 1940, before rather than after entering the war. At that time the Germans were, however, so sure of victory without Spanish help that they did not think they needed it. When Berlin changed its mind on this point six weeks later,[27] Franco was beginning to see that the war might be far from over, and hence quite possibly no longer worth joining.

As even these brief comments should show, the powers associated with Germany were motivated by the shared emotion of greed—as the opposing alliance would eventually be joined by the shared emotion of fear—but very little else. Germany, Italy, and Japan were tenuously allied like a gang of thieves, each out to steal what it could from whichever victim looked most vulnerable at the moment, but without much inclination to defer, or even give much thought, to the needs, hopes, or intentions of the others.

As the war continued, the focus of the fighting shifted repeatedly. First it was in the sky over England where the German air force received a narrow but decisive setback; and in a reversal of the usual procedure in war, the winning rather than the losing commander was sacked.[28] The

27. The relevant works on German-Spanish relations regularly mention the Spanish approach of June 19 and the non-committal German reply of June 25, followed a month later by increasing German interest in an attack on Gibraltar and later willingness to make promises to Spain, but they do not examine this most important alteration in Berlin's position. See Donald S. Detwiler, *Hitler, Franco und Gibraltar: Die Frage des Spanischen Eintritts in den Zweiten Weltkrieg* (Wiesbaden: Steiner, 1962); and Charles B. Burdick, *Germany's Military Strategy and Spain in World War II* (Syracuse: Syracuse University Press, 1968). Andreas Hillgruber's *Hitlers Strategie: Politik und Kriegführung 1940-1941* (Frankfurt am Main: Bernard & Graefe, 1965), follows the account of Detwiler.

28. A full study of the career and shameful treatment of Air Chief Marshall Sir Hugh Dowding remains to be written. Robert Wright, *The Man Who Won the Battle of Britain* (New York: Scribner, 1969), is helpful but one-sided and written before ultra materials became available. Some new light on the dismissal is in Lewin, pp. 87-90. In view of widely held beliefs about the respective roles of Stanley Baldwin and Winston Churchill in Britain's military posture, it is perhaps worth noting that the victor of the Battle of Britain was appointed to his position under the former and dismissed under the latter.

war subsequently centered in the winter of 1940-41 on the Mediterranean, East Africa, and Southeast Europe as the British and then the Greeks defeated the hapless Italians; only German intervention rescued Mussolini from at least some of his follies. The critical fighting after the Battle of Britain, however, was on and under the Atlantic, and in this the British though at terrible cost to themselves won at least a partial victory in 1941. The sinking of the *Bismarck* and the bombing of the new German naval base at Brest on the French Atlantic coast were the most visible signs of possible victory in the *surface* portion of the Battle of the Atlantic;[29] the desperate peril under water remained.[30]

It was precisely to assist with this battle that Germany was so eager to have Japan join in the war against England. Not only would this mean an added drain on British naval resources, but it would divert the United States from any support of Britain in this key theater while the German campaign in Russia temporarily required the reallocation of German resources from sea to land warfare. It was with this in mind that Hitler in the spring of 1941 promised to join Japan in war against the United States, hoping that such a commitment would remove the doubts and hesitations of Tokyo.

Early in 1941 Hitler's mind and the thoughts of his associates were primarily filled with schemes to accompany the expected triumph in the East. Here was endless land for settlement after the inhabitants had been largely expelled, killed, or starved to death with only a subservient

29. Not as spectacularly visible at the time but probably of equal long-range importance was the destruction by the Royal Navy of Germany's network of supply and weather-reporting ships in the North Atlantic.

30. The Axis effort in this was hampered by inadequate coordination between German and Italian submarine forces in the Atlantic. Though offered it by the Italians, the Germans declined full control over Italian submarines for fear of then having to accept greater Italian control in North Africa. Note the comments of Admiral Eberhard Weichold, head of the German naval command in Italy, in his manuscript in the Bundesarchiv/Militärarchiv, Freiburg, N 316/1, pp. 41-42.

remnant allowed to eke out its life as slaves assisting the new masters in the exploitation of its agricultural and mineral riches.[31] With the possibility of Jewish emigration drastically reduced by the continuation of the war, a continuation which also made Madagascar inaccessible to the Germans, Berlin now faced a situation in which the invasion of Russia would enormously increase rather than decrease the number of Jews in the area under German control. In view of this, Hitler ordered in March 1941 that as part of the new campaign in the East measures be prepared to kill all Jews in the lands to be conquered, with the murder squads to move in with the troops.[32] Other categories of objectionable people would be murdered in inconceivable numbers at the same time, while millions more were to be left to starve. The attack on Russia would inaugurate a dramatic and bloody phase in the racial restructuring of Europe intended by Hitler and his associates.[33]

The German invasion, launched on June 22, 1941, was to lead to a quick victory. The disposition of the Red Army in Russia's newly acquired territories and Stalin's ignoring of all warnings only facilitated the initial German strategy. Attacking without warning, the Germans would eliminate the huge Russian air force, cut off large parts of the Red

31. The work of Alexander Dallin, *German Rule in Russia, 1941-1945: A Study in Occupation Policy* (New York: St. Martin's, 1957), remains the best introduction to this subject.

32. A study of the *Einsatzgruppen*, as the murder squads were called, is *Die Truppe des Weltanschauungskrieges* by Helmut Krausnick and Hans-Heinrich Wilhelm (Stuttgart: Deutsche-Verlags-Anstalt, 1981). The current status of research on the origins of the murder squads is best reflected in the book by Christian Streit discussed in n. 34, below. A reliable survey of their activities is in Raul Hilberg, *The Destruction of the European Jews* (Chicago: Quadrangle, 1961), chap. 7.

33. The signal contribution of the two leading German scholars of World War II, Hans-Adolf Jacobsen and Andreas Hillgruber, appears to me to lie in their recognition of and emphasis on this characteristic as the key to understanding Germany's role and conduct in the war as opposed to the tendency in West Germany to regard this facet as separable and incidental, and also as opposed to the equally misleading tendency in East Germany to substitute economic for racial ideological factors in discussing these ghastly events.

Army with armored pincers, and penetrate quickly and deeply into a Soviet Union that was expected to collapse under the hammer blows of the German attack. In some ways the reality approximated the anticipation. In a few weeks the Germans went farther than they had in months during World War I, and the deliriously happy German leaders turned in the summer of 1941 to postwar planning as quickly as they had in 1940. The obvious follow-up to the successful campaign in the East would be a pincer move from the North across the Caucasus and from the West across Egypt, as well as via Turkey, into the Middle East, destroying the British position there, breaking up Britain's empire, and adding the oil of Iraq and Iran to that of the Caucasus conquered on the way. The obvious follow-up to the mass murder of the Jews of occupied Russia was the murder of *all* Jews in German-controlled Europe, and like the military projects just mentioned, this too was ordered in those first weeks of fighting in the East.[34] For the future, the German army could be reduced; emphasis would be shifted to the air force and the navy for concentration on the war against England, while the battleship and carrier construction program would be revitalized for the fight against America. In the meantime Japan, which still seemed a bit reluctant to attack England and risk war with the United States, might be inveigled into the war by the back door through the offer of parts of the Russian booty.[35]

34. Christian Streit's superb study, *Keine Kameraden: Die Wehrmacht und die Sowjetischen Kriegsgefangenen, 1941-1945* (Stuttgart: Deutsche Verlags-Anstalt, 1978), demonstrates in detail and with insight how the willingness of the leadership of Germany's army to participate in large-scale murder facilitated and even accelerated the radicalization of this whole process.

35. The otherwise helpful analyses of the question of Japanese intervention in the German-Soviet war by Andreas Hillgruber in *Deutsche Grossmacht- und Weltpolitik im 19. und 20. Jahrhundert* (Düsseldorf: Droste, 1977), pp. 223-52, and by Hosoya Chihiro's piece "The Japanese-Soviet Neutrality Pact" in Morley, pp. 88-114, both fail to call attention to this critical aspect of the issue. It is surely worthy of note that it was

If in 1941 as in 1940 German hopes were dashed and some of the new projects therefore could not be implemented, it was assuredly not because the Germans did not try. In a series of spectacular victories, the German armies defeated more forces and conquered more territory in six months than in three years of World War I. The very fact, however, that there was still fighting after the first couple of months showed that something was going wrong for them. There were, to be certain, problems for them in the increasingly hard fighting itself. The battles on thousands of kilometers of front ground down the German forces, but for the Russians the bravery of their soldiers at the front, however important, was no more the only critical element for them on land in the fall of 1941 than it had been for England in the air and on the sea the year before. The basic issue in each case was one growing out of the structure of society under the impact of war.

The strains of war had dissolved the bonds which had held together the Russia of the Romanovs in 1916-17; and it had been Hitler's calculation that something similar would happen to Stalin's Russia—only more quickly because, Hitler assumed, the former, racially superior, partly Germanic ruling class of the old regime had been destroyed and replaced by what Hitler imagined was an inferior one of largely Jewish Bolsheviks, and because Germany could allocate a higher proportion of her forces to the Eastern theater of war this time. But this assessment proved erroneous. The British had held together in 1940; the Russians were held together in 1941 by a system that, however much weakened by the crushing blows suffered at the front and the first signs of panic in the interior, still commanded the support of a large population and the apparatus designed to control and mobilize it, tasks greatly facilitated by what the country's inhabitants quickly learned

---

when he thought the Soviet Union defeated—as opposed to the time either before the attack on Russia or after the setbacks on the Eastern front—that Hitler urged Japan to join that portion of the war.

of the murderous policies of the invader who soon turned any possible sympathizers into foes. As the British had been assisted in their ordeal by the strategic advantage of a large water barrier between them and the Germans, so the Russians were assisted by the strategic advantage of being able to concentrate on one front against an enemy who could not do the same. While the Germans could never again after 1940 put all of their effective striking forces on one front, the Soviet Union alone of the major belligerents could do so as they knew of Japan's planned move South. We never know afterward just what the margin was—when it is all over we are so much smarter, knowing how it came out and often overlooking how close the alternatives may have been. But the Russian front held, and the war in the East continued.

Of the countries observing the dramatic events in the war between Germany and the Soviet Union, none watched with greater interest than Japan. The Japanese had themselves had occasion in border fighting in 1938 and 1939 to discover the fighting quality of Soviet arms, and many of them never expected the Soviet Union to fall apart as the Germans did. Anticipating that neither of the antagonists could completely crush the other, they assumed that at some point a new agreement would be reached between them. The obviously desperate situation of the Soviet Union in the summer and fall of 1941, however, reinforced the position of those in Tokyo who argued that now, if ever, was the time for Japan to move. If she did not, the opportunity would probably never recur. Southeast Asia open to attack; the Russians unable to move on land or to allow America to utilize the Russian air bases so threateningly close to the home islands; the United States herself busy in the Atlantic, trying to help Britain and Russia and in any case unprepared as yet—when would so many lights again be green? The passage of time could only make the situation worse: either an end of the war or the completion of American rearmament, to say nothing of both, would be fatal to Japanese ambitions, and neither contingency could be prevented by a non-participating Japan.

Misreading both the likely attitude of the Americans and their own long-term susceptibility to submarine blockade, the Japanese looked only at the easy loot dangling before their eyes. The Japanese did not believe that they could completely defeat America, but if the United States fleet could be removed from the flank of Japan's advance and South and Southeast Asia conquered, a new status quo could then be attained by a new settlement in the Pacific. The Americans would never pay the price in blood and treasure to reconquer places of which they had never heard just so that these could be returned to their former colonial masters, especially when the Americans planned to give up anyway the only important ones they had ever owned themselves. An accommodation in the Pacific, as in Europe, would leave the Japanese, as it would leave their German ally, in a vastly stronger position. Having assured themselves that the German promise to join them in war with the United States still held, they moved south as they had long planned, with the addition of a naval air strike at Pearl Harbor to shield this advance.

The original Japanese plan had called for their submarines to harry the American navy as it moved westward from its bases, and for the main part of the Imperial Navy to send the weakened American force to the bottom of the Pacific with its crews. In the fall of 1941 the surprise attack on Pearl Harbor had been substituted. It seemed to offer a greater assurance of speedy success—even though it would mean a greater opportunity for the survival of many of the American sailors and for the eventual raising and repairing of most of their ships. The very step designed to shield the conquest of Japan's new empire was almost guaranteed to rouse the American people to a point where they would indeed be willing to pay the heavy price of eventual total victory over Japan, thus undermining the whole basis of Japan's strategy for attaining a new and more advantageous situation. In this way, the Japanese opened, as they closed, the general war in the Pacific with what was essentially a kamikaze operation, but this fundamental truth was hidden from their eyes as they rejoiced over their seemingly easy victory over the United States Pacific fleet.

The Germans, who had been trying ever since 1938 to get the Japanese to turn openly against the Western Powers, were delighted by the turn of events. For the only time between 1933 and 1945 Hitler could make a spectacular move—entering the war against the United States--with an essentially unanimous military, diplomatic, and Party hierarchy behind him. In April he had opened his war against Yugoslavia with a surprise Sunday morning air attack—what a sign of brilliance on the part of the Japanese to follow the same procedure! Bolshevism and plutocracy, two sides of the same Jewish coin, could now be crushed simultaneously by those with the courage to strike at the enemies of a new world order.[36]

The difficulties in the land fighting on the Eastern front could now be mastered by Germany under circumstances in which the disadvantages of continued concentration on ground combat were offset by the Japanese move. The losses inflicted on the American and British navies and the demands of war in the far reaches of the Pacific and Indian Oceans on United States and British shipping resources would enable Germany to throttle England in the Atlantic, or at least to hold the situation there until a German victory in the East enabled her to turn full attention to the enemy in the West. For two years the German navy had been begging for war with the United States so that its submarines could torpedo whatever floated wherever it could be found—now they would get the chance.

36. This whole issue is examined in detail on pp. 90-95.

As the Japanese stormed forward to seize their new empire, Germany struck heavily in the Atlantic[37] even as she made ready to strike once again on the Eastern front. The victories of each would hold the prospect of a meeting of their two empires far more substantial than the valuable but ever tenuous Trans-Siberian railway link that the Soviet Union had provided from 1939 to 1941. A Germany triumphant on the southern portion of the Eastern front and in North Africa would meet a Japan moving from conquest in the Pacific to domination of the Indian Ocean. The junction of the Germans and Japanese would separate their enemies, deprive them of the resources of the Middle East when they had already lost those of Southeast Asia, and thus assure a total triumph over these decadent and inferior countries.

The Japanese defeat at Midway at the beginning of June 1942 blunted this procedure in the Pacific, while the American landing in the Solomon Islands in August started a series of battles that would keep the Japanese from carrying the war into the Western part of the Indian Ocean. The British defensive victory at El Alamein at the beginning of July 1942 halted the Axis advance in North Africa, while the Russian defenses in the Caucasus and at Stalingrad held the Germans there in grim battles in late August and early September. There would be no German-Japanese handshake in the Persian Gulf.

The war ground on. Already the British had mounted their first thousand-plane raid at the end of May 1942, and Australian and American troops were beginning their push in New Guinea. But most of the fighting of the war was on the Eastern front. There millions were locked

37. The account of operation "Paukenschlag" off the coast of North America in Holger H. Herwig, *Politics of Frustration: The United States in German Naval Planning, 1889-1941* (Boston: Little, Brown, 1976), pp. 240-41, misses the critical point: the horrendous impact on Allied shipping. See, for example, the comments of Brian B. Schofield, wartime Director of the Trade Division of the British Admiralty, in Rohwer and Jäckel, p. 158.

in the fiercest combat, which ended in death for hundreds of thousands—and never seemed to end at all for the rest. German soldiers involved in this interminable bloodbath put something of their view of it, and the ordinary fighting soldier's attitude toward rank and decorations, into a bitter joke: Germany had finally won in the East, and the great victory parade was being held in Berlin. At the head of the parade strutted Göring, promoted from Reichsmarshall to World Marshall, dressed in plain gold and wearing the Mammoth Cross of the Iron Cross, not just with oak leaf clusters, but with self-propelled laurel trees. There followed a full division of twelve thousand field marshalls stepping by in cadence, and an endlessly glittering array. At the very end of this long procession there was a single Landser, a German GI. Unshaven, wearing a torn uniform, and bowed down under the weight of field pack and assorted equipment, he was indeed an incongruous sight. One of the bystanders asked him what on earth he was doing in this spectacle. The soldier could only shake his head and answer in pidgin Russian, "nix panimayou," I don't understand a thing. He had been on the Eastern front so long, he had forgotten his German.

World War II: The Allies, 1941-1945

A famous story about the late Earl Mountbatten describes his demonstration of the strength of Pykrete to a group of skeptical high-ranking officers examining the latest brainchild of his Combined Operations Command. Pykrete was a frozen mixture of seawater and sawdust. A block of ice and a block of Pykrete were brought in; Mountbatten fired his revolver at each in turn. The ice shattered, but when he fired at the Pykrete, the bullet bounced off and ricocheted around the room. Lord Louis was not asked to repeat the demonstration. Why Pykrete and what for? For Habakkuk, the code name of the project to provide air protection for the invasion of France and for convoys in the Atlantic. Habakkuk was to be a floating airport, two thousand feet long and three hundred feet wide, constructed of Pykrete sheathed in wood, driven by outboard motors for up to seven thousand miles and carrying two hundred planes. As other ways were found to cope with the needs this project had been designed to meet, Habakkuk was scrapped from the arsenal of the Allies—though happily not from the Bible—while its equally outlandish companions, the huge artificial harbors to supply the invasion forces, called "Mulberries," were being constructed in England to be dragged across the Channel for emplacement off the Normandy coast.[1]

Resort to these extraordinary devices underlines the fundamental strategic difference in the position of the Allies vis-à-vis the Axis, especially Germany. The Soviet

1. The story of Habakkuk is summarized in Bernard Fergusson, *The Watery Maze: The Story of Combined Operations* (New York: Holt, Rinehart & Winston, 1961), pp. 145-46, 287, 289, 298-99.

Union's defensive position was extremely bad: having itself arranged for a long direct land border with Germany, and having simultaneously driven into Germany's open arms Finland and Rumania, the countries at the northern and southern extensions of that border, Russia was open to invasion from the West, an invasion made all the easier by the partial dismantling of the fortifications on the old border and the stationing of large forces in the newly acquired lands. The converse of this dangerous defensive position was, of course, that if the Germans were once held on that front, the Red Army would be in a fine position strategically for the offensive. The land mass of Eastern Europe could potentially serve as an avenue for invasion westwards as well as eastwards. As Germany could bring her military power to bear directly on the Soviet Union, so the Soviet Union could bring hers to bear directly on Germany.

The situation of Britain and the United States was the exact opposite.[2] In the face of Germany's initial offensives, England had the defensive advantage of a very wide moat—without any drawbridge.[3] Attack would have to be launched against her by air and sea, both vastly more difficult than attack on the ground; and we have already seen that the Germans thought a land attack in the East easier and less risky than a seaborne invasion in the West. Similarly, the oceans protected the United States from direct and easy

2. It is on this point that so much of the German literature on World War II, even the best, is defective. Note the erroneous generalization that the "allied coalition could operate from a far superior strategic position," with no sense of the obvious geographic differentiation, in Hans-Adolf Jacobsen, *Zur Konzeption einer Geschichte des Zweiten Weltkriegs 1939-1945* (Frankfurt am Main: Bernard & Graefe, 1964), p. 44, reprinted in his *Von der Strategie der Gewalt zur Politik der Friedenssicherung* (Düsseldorf: Droste, 1977), p. 60.

3. Although it contains interpretations with which I cannot agree, the book of Walter Ansel, *Hitler Confronts England* (Durham, N.C.: Duke University Press, 1960), seems to me particularly valuable for the way in which the author, a retired Rear Admiral of the U.S. Navy, has integrated the naval aspect and issues of amphibious warfare into the discussion of German planning and operations in 1939-40.

enemy attack: the shells of a Japanese submarine fired off the California coast and the unmanned incendiary balloons landing in the Pacific Northwest only underline the difficulties facing a potential invader with serious hopes of success. The German landings on the Channel Islands and the Japanese landings in the Aleutians, both of which tied down Axis resources in unprofitable sideshows, similarly illustrate the enormous defensive advantages of the position of England and the United States in the face of the Axis offensive.

But German-controlled Europe was separated from British and American military power by the same waters which had protected the United Kingdom and the United States, and the advantage for defensive strategy thus constituted a great disadvantage for any attempt to turn to the offensive. This great difference between the positions of the allies of World War II—which was *not* the case in World War I—is so obvious that it has generally escaped the notice of historians, especially the Germans and Russians. It presented the Western Allies and the Russians with entirely different sets of problems. These differences, furthermore, interacted with the different approaches pursued by the major powers of the Tripartite Pact. Germany combined a primarily offensive strategy on land with a turn to the defensive at sea, while Japan launched her offensive at sea and then turned to a defensive strategy on land.

To the fundamentally different strategic positions of the Allies must be added an equally striking difference in the military realm. The military postures and power of the three main allies were entirely dissimilar. Britain faced rigid limits on her human resources, mobilized to an extraordinary degree, as she had lifelines to protect around the globe and no way to get back at the Germans except by air. Her military effort, therefore, had to be concentrated at sea and in the air with the result that her army, even as it was laboriously rebuilt and reequipped after initial military disaster, always remained limited in size.[4] It became fashionable during the war—and at times this foolishness recurs in the literature—to berate the British for not being sufficiently enthusiastic about a massive invasion of Western Europe until success could be considered at least a reasonable possibility, but the realities of manpower set their own inexorable limits. Twice before the British had been driven off the continent (while the Soviet Union provided assistance to the Germans); they could hardly risk another disaster. In the event, after less than three months of fighting in France in 1944, even before the liberation of Paris, the first British division had to be pulled out of the front and disbanded so that adequate replacements would be available to keep other units up to strength.[5]

The Soviet Union, on the other hand, had substantial manpower reserves even after massive initial losses and the occupation by the Germans of important areas with their population. A large army had been built up earlier, and the successors and survivors of the purge process of the

4. Well into the war the British army was also hampered by some truly extraordinary incompetence among its generals. This sensitive subject, symbolized by the surrenders of Singapore and Tobruk in 1942, awaits its historian; it should perhaps be seen in conjunction with the high regard, otherwise not easily understood, in which General Montgomery came to be held.

5. Lionel F. Ellis, *Victory in the West,* 1: *The Battle of Normandy* (London: H.M. Stationery Office, 1962), p. 453. Note also the entry in the diary of General Eisenhower's naval aide for July 24, 1944:

> Meanwhile friends at [British] Naval Headquarters [in charge of theater ports and operations] said they felt that Monty, his British Army Commander, Dempsey, the British corps commanders, and even those of the divisions are so conscious of Britain's ebbing manpower that they hesitate to commit an attack where a division may be lost. To replace the division is practically impossible. When it is lost, it's done and finished. Even naval ratings, Air Force personnel, and nondescripts are being "cannibalized" for replacements.

Harry C. Butcher, *My Three Years with Eisenhower* (New York: Simon and Schuster, 1946), p. 622.

1930's provided a considerable core of officers.[6] Russia's air force was large in spite of calamitous losses from the German surprise attack, due to a large aircraft industry and short flight distances at the front, while the navy was small and necessarily scattered. Aided by the fact that alone among the major belligerents they could concentrate military resources on one fighting front, the Russians rebuilt their land power even as they paid with huge losses for past diplomatic and military miscalculations.

American military power when World War II began was limited to the navy, substantial in size but hardly adequate for one ocean, to say nothing of two. The air force existed mainly in theory; while the army was, as indicated in the preceding essay, so tiny as to suggest that a war with Luxembourg was believed by the American public to be the most likely contingency. Naval and airplane construction began to be accelerated in 1940 and 1941, but it would be years before massive results could be attained. Building up an army of meaningful size would be at least as lengthy an undertaking. When serious planning began in the summer and fall of 1941 on what came to be called the "Victory Program," it was anticipated that July 1, 1943, was the earliest time when a real force might conceivably be available for service. Whether the needed equipment and experienced staffs would also be available by then was at least an open question. Ironically, the *Chicago Tribune* published the plan for the benefit of the American public—and the Germans,[7] Japanese, and Russians—a few days before the Japanese attack on Pearl Har-

6. The best general introduction remains John Erickson, *The Soviet High Command* (London: Macmillan, 1962). An excellent introduction to the impact of the purge on the Red Army is Seweryn Bialer (ed.), *Stalin and His Generals: Soviet Military Memoirs of World War II* (New York: Souvenir Press, 1969), pp. 63-88.

7. For German evaluations of the American plans revealed in this security leak, see Michael Salewski, *Die deutsche Seekriegsleitung, 1935-1945*, 3 (Frankfurt am Main: Bernard & Graefe, 1973), pp. 235ff. (the full text of the High Command of the Armed Forces [OKW] study cited there is in Bundesarchiv/Militärarchiv, PG 32225, P-379).

bor made certain that the program would indeed be carried out.

All this meant that in the first years of American participation in the war, there could be no major United States role in the fighting, at least on land. Hard experience would show that it took almost twenty-two months to get a division ready for overseas duty.[8] If Germany and Japan went to war with the United States in 1941 unafraid of the American army, it was because neither, with good reason, thought of itself as militarily in a class with Luxembourg.

To these differences in the strategic positions and military posture of the allies must be added a third fundamental differentiation: the political one. It was not only that their political and social systems and structures were so different, and that their ways of doing things were so dissimilar, but that the broad aims with which they had entered and continued in the war had rather little in common. Great Britain had come into the war in accordance with an obligation to Poland assumed in the belief that Germany could be restrained or defeated only by a coalition of those threatened by her expansionist aims. The British fought on to defend themselves, to protect their empire from those expecting to steal it, and to recreate some sort of balanced system in Europe, or at least the western and central portions of it, with a restored France as a key element. Reduced by economic and military factors to an increasing dependence on the United States, the British might hope someday to regain a full independence from that friend for themselves;[9] but in any case, they would continue to fight it out with Germany alongside whatever allies could be found in a desperate struggle

8. Forrest C. Pogue, *George C. Marshall. 3: Organizer of Victory* (New York: Viking, 1973), p. 493.

9. Before the war, on September 21, 1938, the British Undersecretary of State for Foreign Affairs, Sir Alexander Cadogan, had commented: "Pray God we shall never have to depend on the Soviet, or Poland or—the U.S." (PRO, FO 371/22276, N 4601/533/63).

which they had entered hardly recovered from their prior bout with the same foe.

The Soviet Union had tried hard to stay out of the war altogether and had failed. The Soviets had almost slithered into the war on Germany's side during the 1939-40 winter war with Finland.[10] They had been able to avoid further entanglement in Scandinavia first by making a major concession to the Finns in the north, returning Petsamo with its port and nickel mine to Finland after occupying the area during the fighting,[11] thereby leaving a buffer between themselves and Norway; and second as a result of Germany's invasion of Denmark and Norway. Dragged into the conflict by German invasion, Russia defended herself as best she could.

Stalin's hope appears to have been to get out again with minimum cost and maximum gain, letting the others resume fighting each other as they had before and might again. On the one hand Russia would fight hard to maintain herself, regain the earlier loot, and maybe add to it. On the other hand, there was the possibility that some-

10. During the winter of 1939-40, the Western Powers considered a number of projects for interfering with Germany's supplies of essential war materials, especially oil and steel. These projects included attacks on Soviet oilfields in the Caucasus and cutting off Swedish iron ore by occupying the mines and/or transport routes as a major part of a mission to aid Finland. Either of these moves, if implemented, would presumably have involved Britain and France in hostilities with the Soviet Union. On the Caucasus plan, see Günter Kahle, *Das Kaukasusprojekt der Alliierten vom Jahre 1940* (Opladen: Westdeutscher Verlag, 1973), and numerous articles by the same author. On the Scandinavian plans, see Sir Llewellyn Woodward, *British Foreign Policy in the Second World War*, 1 (London: H.M. Stationery Office, 1970); and François Bédarida, *La Stratégie secrète de la drôle de guerre: Le Conseil Suprême Interallié, septembre 1939–avril 1940* (Paris: Presses de la Fondation Nationale des Sciences Politiques, 1979).

11. The return of Petsamo and the nickel mine to Finland is discussed in H. Peter Krosby, *Finland, Germany, and the Soviet Union, 1940-1941: The Petsamo Dispute* (Madison: University of Wisconsin Press, 1968), pp. 8-10; it is however missing from the recent account by Michael Salewski, "Staatsräson und Waffenbrüderschaft, Probleme der deutsch-finnischen Politik 1941-1944," *Vierteljahrshefte für Zeitgeschichte*, 27, No. 3 (July 1979), 370-91.

thing very similar might be attained once the front had stabilized either by a separate peace with the Germany of Hitler or with a Germany ruled by military men who looked on good relations with Russia as a proper German policy; and of course either of these procedures would be infinitely cheaper and more certain than fighting it out with Germany to the end. The lines required by this double, or perhaps triple, policy could be pursued and were pursued simultaneously; and if that meant a rather prickly and distant relationship with one's allies, that was their problem, not Stalin's own. Perhaps he assumed that they would act similarly, but in any case does not appear to have cared very much.

The United States had been as unsuccessful in staying out of war by helping Hitler's enemies as Russia had been by helping Hitler. What made matters worse for the Americans was that they had been spectacularly unsuccessful in averting war in the Pacific, as the government had very much hoped would be possible because Germany was seen in Washington as by far the greater danger. The situation that resulted seemed to call for doing the best possible defensive fighting in the Pacific while building up American military might for a defeat of Germany first to be followed by that of Japan, thereby ending the threats on both sides. It was hoped that a restored France in Europe and a revived China in Asia would operate to restrict danger in a future in which some form of international organization, the end of colonialism, and cooperation among the victors would create a peaceful world in which the United States could continue to flourish. Whatever else they required, such aims could only be secured by a fight to the finish against both Germany and Japan. This view was reinforced in the minds of those in charge of American policy by their personal memories of political and diplomatic disaster at the end of the preceding conflict when the repudiation of the Wilson administration, which had overruled the American field commander's advocacy of fighting for unconditional surrender just before the November 1918 election, had been followed by the defeat of Roosevelt as vice-presidential candidate in 1920 and an abandonment of the whole international policy of the administration.

In spite of these three categories of differences, the real possibility of defeat in the war pushed the three Allies together for a while. And because two of the three—Britain and Russia—had no choice but to concentrate on fighting Germany first, the broad outlines of strategic priority were so obvious that even the shadows cast by Admiral King and General MacArthur could not hide them. But the longer the war lasted, the stronger the United States and the weaker Great Britain would become, and the greater the stress imposed by different aims for the future as well as tactics in the present. Thus it would become ever more difficult to hold together the three disparate powers joined by German initiative and Japanese actions into what the head of the U.S. Military Mission to the U.S.S.R., General John R. Deane, appropriately called "The Strange Alliance."[12]

As the Japanese moved from triumph to triumph in the early months of 1942 and the Germans stabilized their lines in Russia in anticipation of new offensives, their prospects looked favorable indeed. The stupendous naval victories of the Japanese seemed likely to reverse the tenuous surface victory of the British in the Atlantic at the same time as German submarines increased their sinkings by wholesale devastation of Allied shipping in their new happy hunting ground off the American East coast. The desperately strained shipping resources of Britain and the United States were further burdened by the vast distances of the Pacific, while their limited escort ships now had to be

12. John R. Deane, *The Strange Alliance: The Story of Our Efforts at Wartime Co-operation with Russia* (New York: Viking, 1947).

stretched for convoy duty in hitherto safe, or almost safe, waters. Reeling under Japanese blows, the forces of the Western Powers were divided between two widely separated theaters—as the Germans had been telling the Japanese for two years.

Even in the one field in which the enemies of the Axis had once held what appeared to be an insurmountable lead, that of basic economic resources, the tide seemed about to change dramatically. The Japanese advance in Southeast Asia would soon deprive the British and Americans of their major sources of rubber and tin, a large proportion of their oil, and substantial other resources as well, while adding these riches to the resources already at the disposal of Germany and Japan. Furthermore, there was the possibility of an even more spectacular shift: a strike by Japan westward across the Indian Ocean meeting a German advance eastward would deprive the Western Powers of Mideast oil, and simultaneously close the Persian supply route to a Russia deprived of her Caucasus oil fields into the bargain.

As the stunning victories of Germany in Western Europe earlier in the war had opened up opportunities for Japan, so the Japanese victories in Asia now opened up new opportunities for Germany. Both powers moved forward in 1942 with great strength and, while the point is easily and conveniently forgotten, with enormous initial success. As has been indicated in the preceding essay, the hopes of the Japanese and Germans were checked at Midway in June, El Alamein in July, and at Stalingrad and in the Caucasus in August and September of 1942. It is, however, quite mistaken to assume that these checks to the Axis immediately opened the way for the defeat of the powers of the Tripartite Pact; quite the contrary. The prior conquests of Germany and Japan added greatly to their strength, and the defensive victories of the Allies opened up a most difficult period in the fighting, surely preferable to the almost endless series of defeats that had gone before, but hardly an easy road.

The Japanese setback at Midway had deprived them of some of their offensive capacity because of the loss of four aircraft carriers, but as the Americans soon discovered in the Solomons, Japan had great naval strength and enormous resilience. The American and Australian naval catastrophe at Savo Island in August 1942 and the desperate fighting on Guadalcanal and in Papua showed that the real war in the Pacific was just beginning to get under way. It would in fact draw more resources from the United States if a whole new series of defeats were to be avoided and if Japan were to be prevented from so consolidating her hold on her newly conquered empire as to make its eventual destruction forbiddingly difficult and costly. The halting of Rommel's advance into Egypt would also pave the way for a subsequent counteroffensive, but the long and bloody road from El Alamein to the Alps never did reveal the "soft under-belly of Europe" so often mentioned before the "light at the end of the tunnel" entered the language of war.

Similarly on the Eastern front, the tremendous Soviet victory at Stalingrad not only brought on a more determined German mobilization of her own military and industrial resources as Berlin finally abandoned the concept of a series of short wars for the reality of an all out conflict, but it also led straight to a military defeat at least as disturbing to the Russians as that at Savo Island for the U.S. Navy. The German victory at Kharkov in the last week of February and the first two weeks of March 1943 could not undo the shock of Stalingrad for Germany's satellites,[13] but it precluded any appearance of overconfidence in the Soviet government.

The Russian feelers for a separate peace with Germany

13. A most helpful study of this issue in Jürgen Förster, *Stalingrad: Risse im Bündnis, 1942/43* (Freiburg: Rombach, 1975).

were pursued especially during 1943, and they ran parallel to the creation by Moscow of the National Committee for a Free Germany and the League of German Officers, recruited from among German prisoners of war and offering the possibility of a German nationalist alternative to Hitler.[14] Stalin's refusal for a long time to associate himself with a call for unconditional surrender reflected his reluctance to commit himself and his country, if there were any alternative course open, to the obviously enormous costs of a fight to the finish with Germany, a fight which would leave Russia terribly weakened for future contingencies. He would, indeed, be prepared for the possibility of having to fight all the way to Berlin, and he would have a regime of German Communists ready to fly in with the Red Army's baggage; but nothing happening on the Eastern front suggested this as a particularly attractive process. As his forces advanced, Stalin appears to have shifted his sights from the borders of 1941 to those of 1914, but working with Germany certainly looked preferable to fighting her—just as it had in prior years. And since the Red Army was engaging the bulk of Germany's land forces, he was less concerned than ever about the troubles of his allies at sea or their efforts in the air.

The Germans and Japanese, accordingly, looked to the war in 1943 without all the hopes—some might say illusions—of 1942, but with every expectation of holding onto most of their earlier great gains, while making the fighting so costly and difficult for their enemies as to assure a split among them or at least a general deadlock. The Japanese held firmly to the perimeter of the huge empire they had conquered, and the minimal American and Australian nibbling at its fringes could as yet be dismissed as of minor importance. The Germans were not only holding in the East and preparing for a new offensive there, but were

14. A useful summary is in Alexander Fischer, *Sowjetische Deutschlandpolitik im Zweiten Weltkrieg, 1941-1945* (Stuttgart: Deutsche Verlags-Anstalt, 1975), chap. 2.

keeping the Allied air attacks away from critical targets and delaying the Allies in North Africa while fortifying the coasts of Western and Northern Europe.

Above all, the German successes against convoys in the Atlantic and in the Arctic Sea off Norway seemed likely to paralyze the Western Powers and thereby disrupt the alliance against themselves, thereby making it possible to return to a process of defeating enemies one at a time. During 1942 the Germans had been able to sink more ships than their enemies had been able to build; and with increasing numbers of submarines going into service, the German navy anticipated a difficult but successful struggle at sea in 1943.[15] It was in part to counter such dangers that the British and Americans announced in public at the beginning of 1943 at Casablanca their basic policy of fighting on until the surrender of their enemies, while in secret placing the war against the submarine menace at the top of their priority list. To secure their North African venture they had made a widely publicized deal with French Admiral Darlan; the announcement of the unconditional surrender policy was designed to reassure their Russian ally and the public at home.[16]

A combination of factors turned the situation around during 1943. On land, the new German offensive in the East was defeated in the great battle over the Kursk salient

15. A recent work by Walter S. Dunn, Jr., *Second Front Now—1943* (University, Ala.: University of Alabama Press, 1980), shifts the turn of the tide in the Battle of the Atlantic from 1943 to August 1942 (pp. 48-53). This transposition helps the argument of the book but hardly alters the realities of the time.

16. See Raymond G. O'Connor, *Diplomacy for Victory: FDR and Unconditional Surrender* (New York: Norton, 1971). The North African campaign itself was in part the result of the need to save shipping by opening the Mediterranean and was partly in turn affected by the shipping shortage. One reason for the inability of the Allies to move quickly to the seizure of Tunisia was that there had not been enough shipping for both troops and equipment; the commanders had opted for troops but were then short of transport. See John D. Millett, *United States Army in World War II, The Army Service Forces; The Organization and Role of the Army Service Forces* (Washington, D.C.: Government Printing Office, 1954), pp. 61, 63.

and then succeeded by the first massive Russian summer offensive, which drove back the Germans on the central portion of the Eastern front. In the war at sea, the building of ships finally overtook the sinkings,[17] and the opening of the Mediterranean made the available shipping more useful by eliminating the wasteful trip around the Cape of Good Hope for many ships. The introduction by the Allies of new ship-borne radio locator devices combined with their breaking of German codes and the greater availability of long range aircraft to defeat the U-boats in May of 1943.[18] In this portion of the war, the insistence of the Japanese on using their submarines in cooperation with the surface fleet rather than in attacks on merchant shipping had long exasperated the Germans;[19] by the time the Japanese began to listen to their ally, General Douglas MacArthur's strategy of bypassing key Japanese strongholds forced the latter to use their submarines for supply purposes.[20] Axis coordination in the war against Allied shipping never matched the coordination of England, the United States, and Canada in their defense of the oceanic supply routes.

We know today that the Germans never succeeded in reversing this turn of the tide in the Battle of the Atlantic, but they certainly tried very hard. New types of submarines were developed. These types were designed to avoid the dangers posed for them by airplanes and escorts and were

17. Construction overtook submarine sinkings in February, all enemy sinkings in July, and all losses in October 1943 (Rohwer and Jäckel, p. 165).

18. Details will be found in Rohwer and Jäckel, pp. 133-201. See also Jürgen Rohwer, *Geleitzugschlachten im März 1943* (Stuttgart: Motorbuch, 1975).

19. Salewski, *Seekriegsleitung*, 2: 298-99, summarizes this issue.

20. The Japanese did have considerable success with submarines against shipping in the Indian Ocean in 1942, but a general reorientation was never accomplished. There is an excellent survey of the subject by Carl Boyd, "The Japanese Submarine Force and the Legacy of Strategic and Operational Doctrine Developed between the World Wars," in Larry H. Addington, et al. (eds.), *Selected Papers from the Citadel Conference on War and Diplomacy 1978* (Charleston, S.C.: The Citadel, 1978), pp. 27-40.

expected to enable the German navy to return to battle in a new submarine campaign.[21] The new German submarines, like all others, were tested and their crews trained in the Baltic Sea, the protection of which from Russian advances thus became a critical element in German strategy on the Eastern front. This element, which too many have disregarded, acquired a particular significance from two interrelated facets of the German conduct of war. The submarine appeared to be a likely vehicle for Germany's return to major offensive blows and was identified as a service with Admiral Karl Dönitz, since early 1943 also the Commander-in-Chief of the German Navy. Dönitz was in close contact with Hitler in the latter capacity and, as an enthusiastic devotee of the Fuehrer, was steadily rising in Hitler's esteem with significant impact on Germany's military effort.[22]

Simultaneously, the Germans were moving forward with other new weapons to recapture the qualitative lead they had once enjoyed. Jet airplanes, pilotless airplanes, long-distance rockets, and other weapons were expected to recover the initiative for Germany. If they failed to do so, it was not because the Allies could field more advanced weapons, but because the great productive system of the Allied powers was pouring out much greater masses of weapons at least as good as those on which the Germans had previ-

21. Salewski, *Seekriegsleitung*, 2: 496-528, summarizes the issues as seen by the High Command of the German Navy. At the same time, of course, the Allies were also working on new projects—like Habakkuk and huge cargo planes like Howard Hughes's "Spruce Goose"—while they were continually strengthening the anti-submarine forces actually engaged in the shipping war. There is a useful introduction to the Canadian role in John A. Swettenham, *Canada's Atlantic War* (Toronto; Sarasota, Fla.: Samuel Stevens, 1979).

22. This rise in Hitler's esteem culminated, as is well known, in Dönitz's designation by Hitler as his successor in 1945. What is not so well known is that Dönitz continued to consider himself as Germany's legal chief of state for years and, during his time in jail at Spandau, may well have been the only person on earth who still believed that Hitler's political testament was legally valid and binding. On this, see Albert Speer, *Spandauer Tagebücher* (Frankfurt am Main: Propyläen, 1975), esp. p. 335.

ously standardized their production, and because these masses of weapons took effect *before* the new and improved German armaments could influence the course of events. But whether or not the Allied coalition against Germany would hold together that long was certainly not obvious in 1943.

The Japanese were not likely to throw up their hands in despair under any circumstances, but they had as yet few reasons to do so even had they been so inclined. It was by now obvious that the Soviet Union would not allow the Americans to use bases in the Russian Far Eastern provinces to attack the home islands. The situation in China was characterized by continuing stalemate, but Japanese military power there was so great that any serious challenge could be met. When the American government for apparent want of better practical alternatives agreed to the project of Chiang Kai-shek and General Claire Chennault to build up an air striking force in Nationalist China, the Japanese could first anticipate and then carry out a crushing offensive that finished Chiang's armies, Chennault's air force, and American hopes. In Burma, the string of Japanese victories had not yet played out and would continue through 1943, generally ignored by Americans then and since, but not therefore unknown to the participants. In the Pacific, the bulk of Japan's new empire was as yet intact; it will not do for historians to concentrate on the glorious evacuation of Dunkirk and pass by Japan's success in evacuating her forces from Guadalcanal in February 1943. And it should be noted that Dunkirk is very much closer to London than Guadalcanal is to Tokyo.

What really caused the powers of the Tripartite Pact such difficulties in 1943 was that their strategic divergence was even greater than that among the Allies and that they were entirely unsuccessful in bridging that divergence. Italy was fading from the scene as a power as her people paid the price for the discrepancy between Mussolini's ambitions and the nation's real might. The Japanese had not initially anticipated total defeat of their enemies but rather a negotiated end to their war. But this they could not get. In the face of powers that would not settle for a new status quo in East Asia more favorable to Japan, the Japanese saw no alternative to an endless holding operation that by its costs might eventually induce a change in the views of their enemies. The Germans, on the other hand, were in the opposite situation. They could have a compromise peace with one of their enemies, Russia, but did not want it. To call off the soundings through Stockholm the argument was used that one of the intermediaries was supposed to be Jewish, but all evidence points to the real reason being Hitler's insistence on German retention of the Ukraine, a claim he well knew Stalin would not and could not allow. Hitler's explanation, given to Joseph Goebbels, his propaganda minister and long-time associate, on September 22, 1943, was recorded by the latter in his diary: "The Fuehrer would prefer negotiations with Stalin, but he does not believe they would be successful inasmuch as Stalin cannot cede what Hitler demands in the East."[23] The German word used in the original is "abtreten," a term always used for the cession of territory.

Neither Berlin nor Tokyo could persuade its partner to change its policy. The Japanese had long been trying to get the Germans to settle with Russia by negotiations and turn all forces against the real enemy, Britain and the United States,[24] and by the end of 1942 Mussolini was adding his weak voice to this suggestion. The Germans simply would not fall in with such projects and did their best, quite unsuccessfully, to explain their reasoning to their

23. Louis P. Lochner (trans. and ed.), *The Goebbels Diaries, 1942-1943* (Garden City, N.Y.: Doubleday, 1948), p. 477.

24. The Japanese had been pointing in this direction even before the German summer offensive of 1942; see *Akten zur deutschen auswärtigen Politik, 1918-1945*, Series E, Vol. 1 (Göttingen: Vandenhoeck & Ruprecht, 1969), No. 250; Vol. 2 (Göttingen: Vandenhoeck & Ruprecht, 1972), Nos. 4, 19, 48, 78.

partners. Berlin in turn was trying to persuade Japan to shift from a holding operation in the Pacific to vigorous strikes at the British and Americans so that those powers could not implement their obvious strategy of concentrating on Germany first only to concentrate on Japan subsequently. Eventually on this issue, as on that of submarine tactics, the Japanese began to come around, but again far too late: when a new offensive, this time against India, was finally launched early in 1944, the British were at last pulling themselves together in Southeast Asia, and the Japanese attack at Imphal and Kohima was decisively beaten back.

The changing course of the war was symbolized by the tide of battle on the Eastern front where the fall of 1943 saw the Germans lose and the Russians reclaim the Ukraine east of the Dnepr, with a winter campaign then carrying the Red Army across that great river. Under the combined pressures of inadequate combat strength and shipping on the one hand, and the need to move somewhere on the other, the Western Allies had invaded Northwest Africa and from there pushed on to Sicily and the Italian mainland, but the harbingers of future offensives were elsewhere. How could the Allies land in France on the land route into Germany, and how could they eventually seize the islands on the watery path to Japan? In August 1942 they tried out their tactics for the former at Dieppe on the French Channel coast, and in November 1943 they tried out their tactics for the latter at Tarawa in the Gilbert Islands. As they assimilated the bitter and costly lessons of these battles, the production of equipment and munitions and the training of the multitude of needed troops went forward in the United States. As for the tensions among the Allies, these were reconciled, at least temporarily, at the Moscow, Teheran, and Cairo conferences in 1943 much more effectively than the divergencies between Germany and Japan.

In German-controlled Europe as in Japanese-controlled Asia the conqueror exploited the conquered, though with a significant difference. While the Japanese, like the Germans, intended only to use the local population for their own purposes, in practice this often meant working with local nationalist opponents of the former colonial power; and in this fashion the Japanese quite unintentionally would leave behind a legacy of national self-assertion along with bitter memories of cruelty and exploitation. The Germans, on the other hand, operated a purely repressive regime, conquering their allies when they could no longer strike effectively at their enemies,[25] and eventually leaving as mementoes of their presence mass graves of hostages, murder factories, and ruins. The two empires were hardly quiet places during their temporary existence. Resistance movements troubled the invader even if their military importance was, on the whole, slight. More direct in their effects were the increasingly devastating bombing raids on Europe, and most effective were the incursions of American submarines in the Pacific which threatened to do to Japan what the Germans had hoped, and still hoped, to do to the United Kingdom.[26]

As Germany continued in the war, the situation from Hitler's headquarters looked as follows at the end of 1943: the potential dangers from Italy's collapse in the summer had been swiftly and effectively averted. The Italians had been as feckless in leaving as in entering the war, and the

25. It should be stressed that a major proportion of German "successes" in the latter part of World War II was attained in operations against Germany's own former allies, Italy and Hungary in particular. Even the Finns would be subjected to such treatment, though in this case the record would be a checkered one with the Finns winning a victory over the Germans by beating off a German effort to seize the island of Suursari (Hogland) in the Gulf of Finland. There is a summary in Earl F. Ziemke, *The German Northern Theater of Operations, 1940-1945* (Washington, D.C.: Government Printing Office, 1959), p. 296.

26. See Wilfred J. Holmes, *Undersea Victory: The Influence of Submarine Operations on the War in the Pacific* (Garden City, N.Y.: Doubleday, 1966).

Germans had not only taken over their occupation zones in France and Southeast Europe, but had stabilized a front in southern Italy against their own original assumption that this would not be possible.[27] It was true that on the two occasions when the Germans had come close to throwing the Allies back into the sea, at Salerno and Anzio, they had been held both times; but the Allies had little to boast about either. Their one great chance in May 1944 would be thrown away by the obtuseness of General Mark Clark, the American commander, so that the German army escaped encirclement and could continue to hold a line across the peninsula. The heavy blows suffered on the Eastern front had driven the Germans back, but the great danger now loomed in the West. Here, however, was also the great opportunity. If the Allied landing could be defeated, Germany would not only be free in the West for that year, since there was no prospect of a renewed attempt being mounted before 1945; but by that year the new types of German submarines would enter service and permanently hold off her enemies on that side, thereby freeing her to concentrate on the East. A revived and reinforced German army which no longer needed to keep substantial forces in the West could then hope to drive back and perhaps even crush an exhausted Red Army.

The success of the Normandy invasion followed soon after by great Russian victories on the Eastern front—and all this simultaneous with the American offensive in the Marianas—showed that a decisive shift of military power had taken place. Hope for Hitler, once escape from the assassination attempt of July 20, 1944, had convinced him more than ever that he was destined to triumph, lay in two critical conditions: the possibility of the Allies' falling apart, and of Germany holding on.

27. A useful collection of details, even if the interpretation is dubious, is in Josef Schröder, *Italiens Kriegsaustritt 1943: Die deutschen Gegenmassnahmen im italienischen Raum, Fall "Alarich" und "Achse"* (Göttingen: Musterschmidt, 1969).

The former condition, the possible disruption of the alliance against Germany, was dramatically illustrated by the contrast between Soviet policy in Poland and British policy in Yugoslavia. As the Polish Home Army rose in revolt against the Germans on August 1, 1944, there was a brief tacit renewal of the old Russo-German alliance against Poland. The Red Army stood aside as the Germans crushed the Poles in two months of fighting. This was not *their* group of Poles, and if the Germans would do Stalin's dirty work for him, that would save him from having to do it himself. The contrast with British policy is instructive. The English had started by supporting Draja Mihailovich in Yugoslavia at a time when the Yugoslav communists, like those elsewhere, were still bound by the Nazi-Soviet Pact. As it became evident in subsequent years, however, that Tito's partisan movement was the more effective opponent of the Germans, London switched support to him and eventually persuaded Washington to go along with this policy.[28] The contrast in priorities was striking: the Cold War would start out of one episode, the disruption of Stalin's East European empire would begin in the other; but the more immediate significance was in the possibility of a split in the alliance against Germany growing out of the Polish dispute.

Before the German attack on Russia, the British had tried to entice Stalin to their side with offers of support for Soviet ambitions in Southeast Europe; after the attack, they tried equally unsuccessfully to convert the United States to a policy of accepting Soviet annexations to the 1941 border. Churchill's famous deal with Stalin on spheres of influence in October 1944 was consistent with this pattern.[29] He would, however, learn that as long as the Soviets

28. A survey is in Elisabeth Barker, *British Policy in South-East Europe in the Second World War* (New York: Harper & Row, 1976).

29. There is a helpful review of the evidence in Albert Resis, "The Churchill-Stalin Secret 'Percentage' Agreement on the Balkans, Moscow, October 1944," *American Historical Review,* 83, No. 3 (April, 1978), 368-87.

had to fight their way every centimeter of the road to Berlin, they intended to control fully each one of those centimeters. With Poland as the outstanding example of friction, the Western and Eastern Allies did appear likely to fall apart as soon as they seemed no longer to be in mortal peril themselves.[30]

As for the second condition, that of Germany continuing to hold on in the West, this was a compound of German strategy and Allied problems. As a new form of the old German strategy of striking at the most vulnerable aspect of Allied power—the problem of trans-oceanic supply—the Germans had either destroyed or continued to hold on to most of the ports on the Atlantic and Channel coasts of France. They thereby created enormous logistical difficulties for the American and British invasion forces, difficulties which eventually, as Hitler anticipated, forced them to slow down as they outran their supplies.[31] After General Montgomery failed to clear the approaches to Antwerp harbor promptly, the Allies gambled on an endrun across the lower Rhine; but the inherent contradiction of a methodical commander trying to undertake a risky operation with safety ended in disaster at Arnhem. The Western Allies had indeed been held, and now it would be Germany's turn.

The German armed forces had added a number of newly

30. The best survey currently available is Vojtech Mastny, *Russia's Road to the Cold War: Diplomacy, Warfare, and the Politics of Communism, 1941-1945* (New York: Columbia University Press, 1979).

31. One of the few surviving complete transcripts of a military conference of Hitler's, that of July 31, 1944, contains a lengthy discussion by him of this strategic concept; it is printed in Helmut Heiber (ed.), *Hitlers Lagebesprechungen: Die Protokollfragmente seiner militärischen Konferenzen, 1942-1945* (Stuttgart: Deutsche Verlags-Anstalt, 1962), pp. 584-609. The effectiveness of this approach is evident from the title of the first portion of Volume 2 of Roland C. Ruppenthal, *United States Army in World War II, The European Theater of Operations, Logistical Support of the Armies* (Washington, D.C.: Government Printing Office, 1959): "The Tyranny of Logistics, September 1944-February 1945." The first chapter of this volume is entitled "Logistic Limitations as the Arbiter of Tactical Planning."

mobilized divisions and considerable equipment.[32] Where would Germany land her one big remaining punch? Hitler had for months been planning what was to be a major blow at the Americans. Here was a chance to get back to the concentration on one front, this time by knocking the Americans about so badly that the weak American home front would come apart under the impact of a decisive defeat in battle, a defeat that would necessarily take the British down too. What Americans came to know as the Battle of the Bulge was launched against them on the assumption that they were the most vulnerable partner in the hostile coalition.

The last hopes of the Germans would fade under the concentric attacks of the unbroken alliance, just patched together again at Yalta, while the last hopes of the Japanese were still strong in the Pacific. There, victory for Japan in China in 1944 seemed at least a partial offset against defeat in Burma; and even the American advance in the Philippines with its major victory over the Japanese navy led only to ever more horrendous fighting on Iwo Jima and Okinawa. The war in the Pacific was escalating dramatically in the very months that the war in Europe wound down. As the Americans concentrated on bombing the home islands of Japan and redeploying troops from Europe to East Asia to take part in the bloody battles anticipated there,[33] and as the British and Australians prepared new offensives in Southeast Asia, the Japanese turned with more determination than ever to so greatly raising the

32. The interaction of Allied logistic difficulties in the East and West with Germany's military recovery in the fall of 1944 remains to be analyzed in a comprehensive way. There is an introduction to the question from the perspective of a portion of the Western front in Hugh M. Cole, *United States Army in World War II, European Theater of Operations, The Lorraine Campaign* (Washington, D.C.: Government Printing Office, 1950), pp. 29ff.; for the Eastern front, see Earl F. Ziemke, *Stalingrad to Berlin: The German Defeat in the East* (Washington, D.C.: Government Printing Office, 1968), pp. 340ff.

33. Aspects of the interrelation of the European and Pacific theaters in 1945 are touched on in Pogue, *Marshall*, 3: 539, 574-75, 583.

cost for the Allies with suicide weapons and operations that they might divert their enemies in the direction of a negotiated peace. When the grim planners in the War Department looked to the invasion of the Japanese home islands, they ordered the construction of a new "Mulberry," a new artificial harbor for support of the March 1946 landing in Tokyo Bay, to be dragged this time across the Pacific to the far shore as such contraptions had been hauled across the Channel to Normandy in 1944. This stupendous project was to be given the highest priority; but to the incredulous surprise of the planners, it came back from the Joint Chiefs of Staff with the notation: "priority above all military and naval programs except Manhattan."[34] What on earth could the usually serious General Marshall mean with this jocular sounding reference to a cocktail?

Years before, fearful of German scientific and industrial skills, Britain and the United States had entered into what they believed was a race with Germany for the construction of an atomic bomb. By the time they discovered in 1944 that the Germans were putting their effort into entirely different new weapons, the Western Allies were on the way to completing their own, anticipating in December of that year that one might be ready by August 1945.[35] As a possible alternative to the even greater horrors that would accompany invasion of the home islands, the first bombs that were ready were dropped on Japan in a manner designed to fool the Japanese into thinking that the United States had an indefinite supply, and hoping thereby to shock them out of pursuit of their existing strategy into surrender. By the narrowest of margins, with the Emperor siding with the peace faction of an evenly divided government and in the face of violent internal Japanese objections to giving in, this tactic worked. The war which had

34. Ray S. Cline, *United States Army in World War II, The War Department, The Operations Division* (Washington, D.C.: Government Printing Office, 1951), pp. 347-48, n. 55.

35. Pogue, *Marshall,* 3: 507.

been expected to last well into 1946 ended in August 1945.

Over the ruins, the victors faced the defeated and each other. Tens of millions had lost their lives in the great disaster, endless millions were, or would soon be, homeless. Ruin and devastation, hunger and disease were the legacy of years of bitter fighting. If the world which emerged from this cataclysm was not bright and shiny, how could anyone claim surprise? The victors had held together and had coordinated their efforts more effectively than the defeated, but with exceedingly aggravating difficulties. Resentments accumulated alongside the successes; the different aims would lead to new arguments once hostilities ceased. The Russians with some twenty million deaths had paid by far the greatest price in blood, only to see the richest prize—the industrial heart of Europe—fall primarily to the control of the Western Powers whose combined fatal casualties had been below one million. The Americans and British in turn saw their hopes for the independence of many European countries shattered by the substitution of Soviet for German domination. The restoration of France and the changing events in China would quickly disappoint whatever aims and prophecies any of the wartime allies had entertained about the postwar roles of these two powers.[36] It was not a happy legacy. Shakespeare had put into Mark Antony's mouth the epitaph: "The evil that men do lives after them; the good is oft interred with their bones." And Hitler's grave was empty.

When Neville Chamberlain, the Prime Minister of Great Britain, the only country which fought from the beginning to the end of both world wars, heard that there was to be a Nazi-Soviet Pact, he correctly believed that this develop-

36. Note the conclusions of R. T. Thomas, *Britain and Vichy: The Dilemma of Anglo-French Relations, 1940-1942* (New York: St. Martin's, 1979).

ment was likely to encourage the German dictator to start a war. He therefore wrote to Hitler on August 22, 1939:

> It has been alleged that, if His Majesty's Government had made their position clear in 1914, the great catastrophe would have been avoided. Whether or not there is any force in that allegation, His Majesty's Government are resolved that on this occasion there shall be no such tragic misunderstanding.
>
> If the case should arise, they are resolved, and prepared, to employ without delay all the forces at their command, and it is impossible to foresee the end of hostilities once engaged. It would be a dangerous illusion to think that, if war once starts, it will come to an early end even if a success on any one of the several fronts on which it will be engaged should have been secured.[37]

But Hitler and his associates would have a war, and like a primitive chieftain of some barbaric tribe he would be buried on a funeral pyre with his servants and vast human sacrifice. The cloud from that pyre hangs over us all.

37. *Documents on British Foreign Policy, 1919-1939,* Third Series, Vol. 7, *1939* (London: H.M. Stationery Office, 1954), No. 145.

Hitler's Image of the United States

A significant factor in the understanding of international relations is the perception of countries and issues by those in a position to make policy. The more policy formulation is restricted to one man or a small group, the more important this factor becomes. The conduct of foreign relations by a dictator can often be understood only by reference to his image of the outside world, an image that acts as a filter distorting the realities he sees. This is particularly true for Adolf Hitler whose views on most matters changed very little during his adult life, and who was little affected by experience which leads other men to adjust erroneous perceptions to facts.

Because of its emphasis on the unearthing of new documentary evidence, the study of diplomatic history has often tended to attempt a reconstruction of events on the basis of knowledge subsequently attained by the scholar though contemporaneously unknown to the actors. Even when allowance for this factor has been made, the information known at any given time is frequently seen only through the eyes of the writer without regard to the perception of that information by the man making the decisions. This attempt to trace Hitler's image of the United States is designed to illustrate an avenue for examining the diplomatic history of the recent past. This essay, therefore, will be no survey of German-American relations, but an analysis of the particular and personal perspective of Adolf Hitler on the United States and the implications of his image of America for his policies.

"Hitler's Image of the United States" is reprinted here by permission of the *American Historical Review*, where it originally appeared in Vol. 69, No. 4 (July 1964), pp. 1006-21.

Hitler did not leave an extensive correspondence with friends, relatives, and officials, which might provide a basis for assessing his attitudes. Nor, to judge by available evidence, did he make marginal comments on papers submitted to him for information or decision. He left two books, a few memorandums, a small number of private documents. All the rest consists of public speeches and private talk, recorded by others; even the books are really speeches reduced to writing and provided with some continuity. Since Hitler never earned a reputation for excessive veracity, the scholar faces the question of the reliability of his evidence.

There is a rule of thumb that can be used to good advantage. Before 1933 Hitler talked and wrote to gain understanding and support. Blunt, outspoken, and revealing to an extent he later regretted, this evidence of Hitler's views can generally be taken as accurate. After 1933 he was confronted with the concrete problems of a man in power and used his public utterances for tactical purposes, mixing open expressions of his views with deception to suit the occasion. From 1933 on, therefore, it is safer to depend on his secret directives and confidential talks to his friends, associates, and officials. Though at times concealing his thoughts even from those closest to him, he was, nevertheless, an inveterate talker who continued behind closed doors the practice of speaking rather openly that he had once started in the Vienna home for men. Where these sources fail us, the plans initiated in accordance with directives then secret, but now known to us, can be used to fill the remaining gaps.

During the First World War and the years immediately thereafter, Hitler appears to have given little thought to the United States. Like that of many German youngsters then and since, Hitler's youthful imagination had once been fired by Karl May's novels about American Indians,[1]

1. *Hitler's Table Talk, 1941-1944,* ed. Hugh R. Trevor-Roper (London:

but Hitler's world in the first years of his political activity hardly extended beyond the Atlantic. As one student of the earliest National Socialist concepts of foreign policy has concluded: "The astounding narrowness of his horizon is also evidenced by the fact that Hitler hardly noticed a world power like the United States of America."[2] Interested like so many Germans in explaining that Germany had really won the war, rather than trying to understand its defeat, he paid no particular attention to American matters beyond constantly repeating the condemnations of President Wilson that were then fashionable in Germany. It is true that one of Hitler's traveling fund raisers went to Detroit in 1924 to try to obtain money from Henry Ford, who had attracted National Socialist attention by his anti-Semitic publications, but Ford turned him down.[3] Although dealing at length with questions of foreign policy, Hitler's first book, *Mein Kampf*, published originally in two volumes in 1925-1926, contains only some incidental references to the United States in its 782 pages. Nevertheless, something has to be said about this book, since Hitler's later views of the United States were, so to speak, grafted onto the schemes and visions propounded therein.

Mixing a crude simplification of social Darwinism with authoritarian views, a general inversion of historical reality, and some fantasies about the Germans and other peoples, Hitler expounded a world view based on the assumption that Germans were somehow superior to all others. They would maintain their superiority first by eliminating the allegedly alien Jewish element in their midst, and second

---

Weidenfeld & Nicolson, 1953), pp. 316-17 (entry for Feb. 17, 1942); compare p. 707 (June 15, 1943).

2. Günter Schubert, *Anfänge nationalsozialistischer Aussenpolitik* (Cologne: Verlag Wissenschaft und Politik, 1963), p. 65.

3. Kurt G. W. Ludecke, *I Knew Hitler* (New York: Scribner's, 1937), pp. 192-201; Ernst Hanfstaengl, *Hitler, The Missing Years* (London: Eyre & Spottiswoode, 1957), p. 41. On Ludecke, see Roland V. Layton, Jr., "Kurt Ludecke and *I Knew Hitler:* An Evaluation," *Central European History,* 12, No. 4 (Dec. 1979), pp. 372-86.

by assuring themselves of adequate space on which to live and proliferate as farmers. This meant the conquest of space in Eastern Europe. The people in that space would be killed or expelled: the soil, not the people, was to be Germanized. Since this program would require war with Russia, the fact that the Communists had taken over in that country was a stroke of good fortune in Hitler's eyes because they had removed the only element in Russian society, the allegedly Germanic state-forming upper class, that might have made for effective opposition. Before this war could be launched, however, it would be necessary to make war on the eternal enemy France, a venture in which Italy and possibly Great Britain were expected to participate. There was thus a threefold program: first, an internal division of Germany into those Hitler considered the real Germans and those who could not qualify; second, a war against France; and third, after that war had freed Germany from the threat to its rear, a war against Russia. This program, expounded at length in *Mein Kampf,* was also the main theme of Hitler's public speeches in the 1920's. With politics as his full-time occupation, he preached this same set of ideas in every town where he could find listeners—listeners, it may be added, who paid to hear this nonsense expounded.

A few years later, in the summer of 1928 as is now known, Hitler dictated a second book. Since in that manuscript there are very extensive references to the United States, one must first examine the factors that seem to have drawn his attention to the subject. What evidence there is suggests that his interest in economic and industrial development, and particularly the automobile industry, was in large part responsible. The years since the writing of *Mein Kampf* had been good, economically. German production, employment, and income were rising substantially, and Hitler, whose political chances were hardly helped by this fact, gave the subject some careful thought. In the first place, the availability of a large land area now appeared to him to have industrial as well as agricultural advantages for the people living there. This was illustrated by the second factor: the conspicuous presence of large numbers of American automobiles in Germany. Always intrigued by things connected with roads and motor vehicles,[4] Hitler was greatly impressed by the fact that in spite of its high wages and great distance, the American automobile industry was so obviously successful in the European market. This was owing, he thought, to America's great space, resources, and domestic market.[5]

Once the United States had caught his attention, the whole apparatus of Hitler's racial determinism had to be applied to explaining that country. Somehow it had to be integrated into his view of the universe. His analysis was as follows: The United States was the product of emigration from Europe. Who had emigrated? Always the most restless, those with the greatest initiative, and therefore the best in each country. Who were the best in each country? Why, of course, the Nordic element. The United States was, therefore, the great meeting place of the Nordics, who were protecting their racial purity by excluding Asiatics and by other immigration legislation. This legislation had previously caught Hitler's attention as shown by one of his earliest reported references to the United States and in *Mein Kampf*.[6] Far from being the melting pot Americans imagined it to be, the United States was in fact a homogeneous country, a gathering in of the finest Nordic racial

4. Hanfstaengl, p. 44; Paul Kluke, "Hitler und das Volkswagenprojekt," *Vierteljahrshefte für Zeitgeschichte*, 7 (Oct. 1959), pp. 341-83.

5. *Hitlers Zweites Buch, Ein Dokument aus dem Jahr 1928*, ed. Gerhard L. Weinberg (Stuttgart: Deutsche Verlags-Anstalt, 1961), p. 123; *Adolf Hitler in Franken, Reden aus der Kampfzeit*, ed. Heinz Preis (Nuremberg, 1939), p. 96. For later references to the same subject, see *Hitler's Table Talk*, pp. 279, 415 (entries for Feb. 2 and Apr. 9, 1942).

6. Hitler's speech of Dec. 10, 1919, in "Hitler als Parteiredner im Jahre 1920," ed. Reginald H. Phelps, *Vierteljahrshefte für Zeitgeschichte*, 11 (July 1963), p. 290; Adolf Hitler, *Mein Kampf* (2 vols., Munich: Eher, 1933 printing), vol. 2, p. 490.

stock from each European country. This not only explained why Americans had made such good use of their living space; it also led to the conclusion that they were exceedingly dangerous people. With a racial headstart over everyone else—especially the European countries drained of their best blood by the same process that had made America strong—and with a vast living space on which to proliferate, the Americans were the real threat to German predominance in the world. Hitler's deduction from this analysis was simple: only a Eurasian empire under German domination could successfully cope with this menace. A third war was now added to the original two. After the first two wars had enabled it to construct a continental empire from the Atlantic to the Urals, Germany would take on the United States. One of the major tasks to be performed by the National Socialist movement, therefore, must be the preparation of Germany for this conflict.[7]

In the years between 1928 and 1933 Hitler was engaged in the bitter struggle for power in Germany, a struggle that he won, but that hardly allowed him much time for reflection on areas in any case peripheral to his major concerns. During the long and violent 1929 campaign against the Young plan, for example, Hitler referred to the United States only once, repeating his views about the combined effects of emigration from Germany and the selectivity of American immigration policy.[8] All his attention was focused on immediate domestic problems. The next period for which there is again evidence on his thoughts about the United States is the time immediately following his assumption of power. Since in the years 1933-1934 and during the subsequent decade his evaluation of the United States was entirely negative, by contrast with the analysis

7. *Hitlers Zweites Buch,* ed. Weinberg, pp. 123-32. The discussion of Hitler's view of the United States in Konrad Heiden, *Der Fuehrer* (Boston: Houghton Mifflin, 1944), pp. 321-25, is based on Hitler's speeches of this period, which contain many messages similar to those in the second book.

8. Hitler's concluding speech at the *Reichsparteitag* on Aug. 5, 1929, *Völkischer Beobachter,* Aug. 7, 1929.

just presented, an effort must be made to explain this reversal. Once again the evidence indicates that the economic situation affected Hitler's thinking. The world depression was on everyone's mind, and it was a prominent subject of international negotiations. Hitler himself was invited to go to Washington to discuss the forthcoming London World Economic Conference, but declined and sent Hjalmar Schacht instead.[9] It is clear, however, that Hitler was tremendously impressed by the fact and impact of economic depression in the United States. This came to be one of his favorite topics and a major theme of National Socialist propaganda. While it is true that the United States recovered from the depression more slowly than other industrial countries, Hitler was still talking about the supposed thirteen million unemployed in America well into the 1940's.[10] He saw the movie *Grapes of Wrath* several times and assumed that it represented the whole United States for all time.

This new perspective required a new analysis in terms of Hitler's racial fantasies. He now concluded that the United States was a racial mixture after all—a mixture from all over, including Negroes and Jews, and what were undoubtedly the inferior exiles from every country except Germany. This mongrel society, in which the scum naturally floated to the top, could not possibly construct a sound economy, create an indigenous culture, or operate a successful political system. No wonder they were thrown into a panic by Orson Welles's reports on the arrival of invaders from Mars.[11] The only hope in America's past had been smashed when the wrong side won the Civil War. As Hitler put it:

9. Gerhard L. Weinberg, "Schachts Besuch in den USA im Jahre 1933," *Vierteljahrshefte für Zeitgeschichte* 11 (Apr. 1963), pp. 166-80.

10. See *Hitlers Tischgespräche im Führerhauptquartier 1941-1942*, ed. Gerhard Ritter (Bonn: Athenäum, 1951), p. 163 (entry for June 3, 1942).

11. *Hitlers Lagebesprechungen: Die Protokollfragmente seiner militärischen Konferenzen 1942-1945*, ed. Helmut Heiber (Stuttgart: Deutsche Verlags-Anstalt, 1962), p. 548.

This is the last death-rattle of a corrupt and outworn system. . . . Since the Civil War, in which the Southern States were conquered against all historical logic and sound sense, the Americans have been in a condition of political and popular [i.e., racial] decay. In that war, it was not the Southern States, but the American people themselves who were conquered. In the spurious blossoming of economic prosperity and power politics, America has ever since been drawn deeper into the mire of self-destruction. . . . The beginnings of a great new social order based on the principle of slavery and inequality were destroyed in that war, and with them also the embryo of a future truly great America that would not have been ruled by a corrupt caste of tradesmen, but by a real *Herren*-class that would have swept away all the falsities of liberty and equality.[12]

If this was what had happened to America's past, the only hope for its future lay in the German element that might someday take over. To quote Hitler once more: "The German component of the American people will be the source of its political and mental resurrection."[13]

This analysis in turn led to different conclusions. The United States was hopelessly weak and could not interfere in any way with the realization of Hitler's plans. Deprived by its racial decomposition of the ability to produce an effective military force,[14] it would eventually fall naturally within a German empire that would also include Mexico (in which Hitler was interested because of the oil resources),[15] and such portions of South America as caught his fancy. In this process, the German-Americans as well as those of German descent in Latin America could play

12. Hermann Rauschning, *The Voice of Destruction* (New York: Putnam, 1940), pp. 68-69.

13. Ibid., p. 70.

14. Ibid., p. 71. On Rauschning's book, see Theodor Schieder, *Hermann Rauschnings "Gespräche mit Hitler" als Geschichtsquelle* (Opladen: Westdeutscher Verlag, 1972).

15. For a summary of German efforts to obtain oil concessions in Mexico, see *Oberkommando der Kriegsmarine*, "A IV Nr. 1813, Betr. Ölversorgung der Kriegsmarine," Apr. 29, 1940, Nuremberg Doc. 984-PS.

an important role if they would only awake to their true destiny.[16]

Thus Hitler went forward in the 1930's unconcerned about and generally uninterested in the United States.[17] In Hitler's secret memorandum on the Four-Year Plan, written in the summer of 1936, as in the famous Hossbach Memorandum on Hitler's revelation of his aggressive intentions in November 1937, there are no references to any possibly significant role that the United States might ever play. In the former, it is passed over as impotent vis-à-vis the Soviet Union; in the latter, it is overlooked as any factor at all.[18] In the spring of 1938, when reminded of American influence in the Far East, Hitler contemptuously asserted that the United States was incapable of waging war and would not dare go beyond empty gestures in international affairs.[19]

These views were undoubtedly reinforced by the continuing underestimation of American military potential by Germany's military leaders in general, and by the German military attaché in Washington in particular. General Friedrich von Bötticher was one of the very few men on whose reporting Hitler ever made a favorable comment,[20]

16. Rauschning, *Voice of Destruction,* pp. 61-64.

17. Louis P. Lochner, *What about Germany?* (New York: Dodd, Mead, 1943), p. 47; see also Joachim Remak, "Hitlers Amerikapolitik," *Aussenpolitik,* 6 (Feb. 1955), pp. 706-14. Hitler later commented disparagingly on Norman Davis, the only prominent emissary of Roosevelt whom he met during those years. (*Hitlers Tischgespräche,* ed. Ritter, p. 87 [entry for May 17, 1942].)

18. The Four-Year Plan memorandum in *Vierteljahrshefte für Zeitgeschichte,* 3 (Apr. 1955), pp. 204-10; the Hossbach Memorandum in *Trial of the Major War Criminals* (42 vols., Nuremberg, 1946-48), 25, pp. 402-13. It should be noted that the German army chief of staff, General Ludwig Beck, in his comments on the Hossbach Memorandum, did call attention to the United States. (Wolfgang Foerster, *Ein General kämpft gegen den Krieg, Aus den nachgelassenen Papieren des Generalstabchefs Ludwig Beck* [Munich: Münchener-Dom Verlag, 1949], p. 63.)

19. Erich Kordt, *Wahn und Wirklichkeit* (2d ed., Stuttgart: Union Deutsche Verlagsgesellschaft, 1948), p. 141.

20. *Hitler's Table Talk,* ed. Trevor-Roper, p. 489 (entry for May 18, 1942).

doubtless because it conformed to Hitler's expectations. Bötticher's reports were not always entirely unreasonable, but they did show the United States in a false light, primarily for three reasons: first, his preoccupation with fantasies about the role of Jews in American life, which fitted perfectly with Hitler's own ideas; second, Bötticher's being somewhat misled by the courtesy that Americans extend to an individual foreigner visiting the country regardless of their attitude toward the country from which he comes; and third, Bötticher's contact with pro-German elements in the American army, and especially with General Douglas MacArthur, then Chief of Staff, whom Bötticher reported as showing great sympathy for German policy in the years 1933-1936.[21]

Public opinion in the United States, and particularly the American press, which showed open disapproval of Germany's racial policies, merely confirmed Hitler's evaluation of American degeneracy. In his eyes, the Americans were not only too stupid to get in out of the rain; they even objected to anyone who did. Furthermore, by racial arithmetic Hitler concluded in November 1937 that the United States was held together by fewer than twenty million Anglo-Saxons,[22] and in November 1938 that there were fewer than sixty million persons of valuable racial stock in the United States.[23] Thus even in regard to population Germany was far ahead, especially after the annexation of Austria and the Sudetenland. It is not surprising

21. Reports of Bötticher, 1933-1936, in German Foreign Ministry microfilm, Ser. 5863, National Archives Microcopy T-120, container 2741, frames E 428919-429450; see, for example, his report on a talk with MacArthur on Aug. 6, 1934 (frames E 429184-87) and the report of May 13, 1935 (frames E 429246-49).

22. Hitler speech of Nov. 23, 1937, in *Hitlers Tischgespräche,* ed. Ritter, p. 443.

23. "Rede Hitlers vor der deutschen Presse, 10 November 1938," *Vierteljahrshefte für Zeitgeschichte,* 6 (Apr. 1958), p. 191. For a sample of this type of arithmetic in the "scholarly" world, see Erwin Zühlke and Erich Michaelsen, "Der Anteil der Deutschstämmigen im Offizierkorps der Vereinigten Staaten," *Deutsches Archiv für Landes- und Volksforschung,* 6 (Dec. 1942), pp. 659-65.

that with such an outlook Hitler was receptive to reports containing the wildest distortions of American reality.[24] Even impressions from America reported by Fritz Wiedemann, his adjutant and long-time associate, could not efface such nonsense.[25]

The negative assessment of America's power potential was further reinforced by the neutrality legislation. These laws, designed to remove what some people thought had been the causes of America's entry into World War I, only encouraged Hitler to start World War II by assuring him that none of his prospective European enemies would be able to secure supplies from across the Atlantic even by purchase. As Hitler was to put it in an exposé for his military leaders: "Because of its neutrality laws, America is not dangerous to us."[26] Contemplating war at a gathering in March 1939, he envisaged a conquest of the United States following the defeat of Britain and France.[27] His cavalier dismissal of Roosevelt's peace appeal of April 1939 thus merely reflected his actual assessment of the power poten-

24. Franz Willuhn (*Reichskanzlei* official) to Joachim von Ribbentrop and Joseph Goebbels, Oct. 15, 1937, *Documents on German Foreign Policy, 1918-1945*, Ser. D (19 vols., Washington, D.C.: Government Printing Office, 1949-), I, No. 416. This document refers to Hitler's great interest in a thirty-six-page report on the United States that lists Senators William Borah, George Norris, and Gerald P. Nye as among the "Reds" allegedly close to Roosevelt, expresses alarm over the appointment of a Negro to the registry of deeds office in the District of Columbia, and warns about the Bolshevization of the American Indians! (German Foreign Ministry microfilm, Ser. 5264, National Archives Microcopy T-120, container 2568, frames E 315836-72.)

25. Ernst von Weizsäcker to Dieckhoff, Jan. 18, 1938, *Documents on German Foreign Policy, 1918-1945*, Ser. D, I, No. 433.

26. Hitler speech of Nov. 23, 1939, *Trial of the Major War Criminals*, 26 p. 331. On the neutrality laws, see Robert A. Divine, *The Illusion of Neutrality* (Chicago: University of Chicago Press, 1962). Hitler's view of neutrality in *Hitlers Zweites Buch*, ed. Weinberg, Chap. 10; also Gert Buchheit, *Hitler der Feldherr* (Rastatt: Grote, 1958), p. 526.

27. William Bullitt to Cordell Hull, telegram 565, Mar. 25, 1939 (State Department Decimal File 740.00/684); Bullitt to Hull, telegram 2050, Sept. 19, 1939, in *Foreign Relations of the United States 1939* (5 vols., Washington, D.C.: Government Printing Office, 1955-57), I, pp. 672-74. This is the report of an alleged participant at the meeting. Internal evidence speaks for the credibility of the account.

tial of the United States. His attempt to ridicule the United States in the public glare of a *Reichstag* session was an echo of his private thoughts.

The outbreak and early course of the war again confirmed Hitler's low assessment of American strength and potential. There is a symbolic coincidence in the fact that right after President Roosevelt's urgent appeal to the belligerents to refrain from bombing civilians, German bombs damaged the residence of the American ambassador to Poland. Confident that isolationist sentiment would keep the United States neutral for some time, Hitler determined to strike in the West quickly.[28] By direct subsidy and special propaganda themes, Germany attempted to strengthen the isolationist elements in America.[29] The pro-Allied sympathies and hopes of a large segment of the American public, on the other hand, had neither brought down any of his dive bombers nor stopped one of his tanks. Surveying the world in triumph after the fall of France in June 1940, Hitler and his associates were confident that they could cope with the United States easily enough. Looking beyond the surrender of Great Britain that appeared imminent to them, they planned to construct thereafter a large navy of battleships that would enable them to move effectively against the United States in the only sphere of power that might present a problem. Simultaneously, the defeat of France seemed also to open the way to German naval bases on and

28. Memo of Hitler, Oct. 9, 1939, *Trial of the Major War Criminals*, 37, p. 472. In explaining to his highest military leaders why Germany should strike in the West soon, rather than wait, Hitler said: "The attempt of certain circles in the United States to lead the continent into a direction hostile to Germany is certainly unsuccessful at the moment but could still lead to the desired success in the future. Here too time has to be seen as working against Germany."

29. Lothar Gruchmann, *Nationalsozialistische Grossraumordnung, Die Konstruktion einer "deutschen Monroe-Doktrin"* (Stuttgart: Deutsche Verlags-Anstalt, 1962); Hans Louis Trefousse, *Germany and American Neutrality, 1939-1941* (New York: Bookman, 1951), pp. 44-45, 110, 133; *Documents on German Foreign Policy, 1918-1945*, Ser. D, IX, Nos. 31, 158, 195, 197, 417, 422, 441, 455, 492, 493, X, Nos. 39, 112, 186, 300, XI, Nos. 2, 721, XII, Nos. 34, 411, 563.

off the coast of Northwest Africa for appropriate use by the prospective battle fleet.[30]

All these prospects were replaced by other plans in the late summer and fall of 1940, as Britain refused to give in. Trying to understand the reasons for such foolhardy unwillingness to acknowledge defeat, Hitler concluded that the British must expect others to fight for them in the future as replacements for the French. Assuming that the Russians and Americans provided this distant hope for England, he decided to take this opportunity to attack Russia. After the German victory in the West, this looked like a simple undertaking that could be accomplished in a few weeks. It would not only destroy Britain's hope of aid from that quarter, but it would immobilize the United States as well. As Hitler put it: "Britain's hope lies in Russia and the United States. If Russia drops out of the picture, America, too, is lost for Britain, because elimination of Russia would tremendously increase Japan's power in the Far East. Russia is the Far Eastern sword of Britain and the United States, pointed at Japan." In other words, once Japan was relieved of the Russian threat at its back door, it would move ruthlessly forward in Asia, thereby keeping the United States occupied in the Pacific.[31]

If the first part of Hitler's speculation proved illusory, in that the war against Russia turned out to be neither as short nor as simple as he had expected, his anticipations about Far Eastern events proved at least partially correct. The collapse or weakening of those European powers with colonial possessions in the Far East encouraged Japan to move southward in the summer and fall of 1940, while the German attack on the Soviet Union in the following year emboldened Japan even more.

30. Fuehrer Conferences on Naval Affairs, July 11, 1940, *Brassey's Naval Annual 1948* (New York, 1948), p. 115; see also the following article.

31. Gerhard L. Weinberg, *Germany and the Soviet Union, 1939-1941* (Leyden: Brill, 1954), pp. 114-17. The quotation is from the Franz Halder diary for July 31, 1940.

It is true that in urging Japan to move forward in Asia, Germany preferred that the Japanese concentrate on Great Britain, while leaving the United States alone for the time being. The Tripartite Pact of September 1940 was in part designed to frighten the United States from intervention in the conflict, but the hasty conclusion of the treaty without regard to the details of the text[32] indicates that the propaganda and publicity role of the pact was more important in German eyes.[33] While the pact negotiations were in progress, Hitler himself explained to his generals that America's armament program would not be effective until 1945,[34] that is, until long after he expected the war to have ended.

The Japanese, however, did not wish to risk moving into Southeast Asia without removing the danger of a threatening American fleet on the flank of their route south. It was under these circumstances that they asked their German and Italian associates in the first days of December 1941 if they too would declare war on the United States if Japan became involved in such a conflict. Although not bound to an affirmative answer by their treaties with Japan, both replied that they would; immediately after Pearl Harbor they did so.[35] The possibility that encouragement of Japan to

32. Johanna M. Menzel, "Der geheime deutsch-japanische Notenaustausch zum Dreimächtepakt," *Vierteljahrshefte für Zeitgeschichte*, 5 (Apr. 1957), pp. 182-93.

33. This is also the view of Theo Sommer's monograph, *Deutschland und Japan zwischen den Mächten, Vom Antikominternpakt zum Dreimächtepakt, Eine Studie zur diplomatischen Vorgeschichte des Zweiten Weltkriegs* (Tübingen: Mohr, 1962).

34. Franz Halder, *Kriegstagebuch, Tägliche Aufzeichnungen des Chefs des Generalstabes des Heeres, 1939-1942*, ed. Hans-Adolf Jacobsen (3 vols., Stuttgart: Kohlhammer, 1962-64), 2, p. 98 (entry for Sept. 14, 1940).

35. Statement by Ribbentrop, Aug. 2, 1945, Files of the Foreign Studies Branch of the Office of the Chief of Military History; Hans Louis Trefousse, "Germany and Pearl Harbor," *Far Eastern Quarterly*, 11 (Nov. 1951), pp. 35-50. The delay of a few days in the German answer, on which Trefousse and others have commented, is easily explained by Hitler's temporary absence from his East Prussian headquarters because of a crisis on the southern part of the eastern front. The moment Hitler returned, he instructed Ribbentrop to give an affirmative answer. Since the Japanese

move south might lead to drastic complications with the United States had been canvassed by Hitler and his associates at least as early as January 1941. Hitler had then considered the risk worth taking, partly because he believed that the economic potential of a German dominated Europe was in any case greater than the "limited possibilities found in Britain and America."[36] In other words, the same step that would trigger Japan's move against Singapore—namely the German invasion of Russia—would provide Germany with the industrial and agricultural prerequisites for dealing with the American intervention that Japan's action might precipitate. On December 4, 1941, the Chicago *Tribune* and Washington *Daily Herald* published major portions of the American "Victory Program," the plan by which the United States hoped to crush Germany if the two countries were involved in war under precisely those circumstances Hitler had postulated. The only effect of this revelation on Hitler was that it provided him with additional material for his speech declaring war on the United States.[37]

It is true that during 1941 Hitler had hoped to postpone war with America. In the spring he had canvassed with Schacht the possibility of the latter's going on a propaganda mission to the United States.[38] Throughout the winter of

---

had not told the Germans the date of the intended attack on Pearl Harbor, the urgency of a reply was not as apparent to the latter as to the former. (See Galeazzo Ciano. *The Ciano Diaries, 1939-1943*, ed. Hugh Gibson [New York, 1946], p. 414 [entry for Dec. 3, 1941]; and *Sekretär des Führers*, "Daten aus alten Notizbüchern," 80, Manuscript Division, Library of Congress.)

36. Fuehrer Conferences on Naval Affairs, Jan. 8-9, 1941, *Brassey's Naval Annual 1948*, pp. 171-72. It should be noted that Hitler welcomed the Russo-Japanese pact of April 1941 as turning Japan from Vladivostok to Singapore (ibid., p. 193).

37. Mark Skinner Watson, *Chief of Staff: Prewar Plans and Preparations* (Washington, D.C.: Government Printing Office, 1950), p. 359 and n. 77, 79; Hitler speech of Dec. 11, 1941, in *Der Grossdeutsche Freiheitskampf, Reden Adolf Hitlers*, ed. Philipp Bouhler (3 vols., Munich: Eher, 1940-42), 3, p. 145; see also Washington *Post*, Jan. 6, 1963.

38. Ulrich von Hassell, *Vom andern Deutschland, Aus den nachgelassenen Tagebüchern, 1938-1944* (Zurich: Atlantis, 1946), pp. 225, 236

1940-1941 Admiral Erich Raeder had urged drastic steps, at the risk of war, against American shipping; Hitler had regularly put him off, preferring to concentrate on the preparations against Russia.[39] On June 21, 1941, the day before the attack on Russia, Hitler had explained that he wanted no incidents with the United States for a few weeks because the success of the invasion would have good effects on Japan and hence on the United States.[40] Even American occupation of Iceland early in July did not shake Hitler's belief that imminent victory in the east would change the whole situation.[41] On July 25 he reiterated his desire to postpone incidents, adding that "after the Eastern Campaign he reserves the right to take severe action against the U.S.A. as well."[42] The eastern campaign continued into the fall of 1941, and Raeder again pressured for drastic steps against American shipping, especially after Roosevelt's shoot on sight order of September 11. Hitler, however, was still convinced that Russia would collapse shortly and that incidents with the United States should, therefore, be avoided until the middle of October.[43] At the beginning of October, he thought that victory had indeed been attained,[44] but by late November, even before the fateful question came from Tokyo, Hitler had already recognized

---

(entries for Sept. 3, Nov. 30, 1941). The reference in Schacht's memoirs is characteristically inaccurate: he places the incident in February, but refers as reason for declining to go to the previous passage of the Lend-Lease Act, which took place in March. (Hjalmar Schacht, *76 Jahre meines Lebens* [Bad Wörishofen: Kindler & Schiermeyer, 1953], pp. 520-21; see also Trefousse, *Germany and American Neutrality*, p. 82.)

39. Fuehrer Conferences on Naval Affairs, Dec. 27, 1940, *Brassey's Naval Annual 1948*, 161, 177 (Feb. 4, 1941), 183-84 (Mar. 18, 1941), 192-93 (Apr. 20, 1941). As early as October 10, 1939, Raeder had been prepared to risk the U.S. intervention he considered inevitable. (Ibid., p. 46.)

40. Ibid., p. 220.

41. Ibid., p. 221.

42. Ibid., p. 222.

43. Ibid., pp. 232-33 (Sept. 17, 1941).

44. Hitler speech of Oct. 3, 1941, in *Der Grossdeutsche Freiheitskampf*, ed. Bouhler, 3, 79; Otto Dietrich, *12 Jahre mit Hitler* (Cologne: Atlas, 1955), pp. 101-102; Rudolf Semmler, *Goebbels—The Man Next to Hitler* (London: Westhouse, 1947), pp. 54-56.

that the war in the east would continue at least into the following year and had informed Joachim von Ribbentrop of his willingness to go to war with the United States.[45] After all, most of Europe was in fact under his control, and as he had just explained to the party's faithful, the European area working for his side already included more than 350,000,000 people compared with America's mere 125,000,000.[46]

Hitler's view was that the United States was really a feeble country with a loud mouth.[47] The Americans were probably doing as much by aiding Britain as they would ever be able to do;[48] thus there was no longer any point in waiting for the United States to intervene at its convenience. There was, furthermore, the danger that Japan might make a deal with the United States if not supported by its allies.[49] In any case, as the German Foreign Minister explained to one of his associates: "A great power does not allow itself to be declared war on; it declares war itself."[50]

All the evidence indicates that the outbreak of war between Germany and the United States left Hitler's view of

45. Oshima Hiroshi to the Japanese Foreign Ministry, Nov. 29, 1941, United States, Congress, *Pearl Harbor Attack, Hearings before the Joint Committee on the Investigation of the Pearl Harbor Attack* (39 vols., Washington, D.C., 1946), 12, pp. 200-202. Hitler spent a few days in Berlin at the end of November in connection with the funeral of General Ernst Udet and a luncheon on November 27 commemorating renewal of the Anti-Comintern Pact. He returned to East Prussia on November 28, following the funeral ceremonies for Colonel Werner Mölders. (*Sekretär des Führers*, "Daten aus alten Notizbüchern," 80.) Oshima was transmitting what Ribbentrop had told him about Hitler's views at that time.

46. Hitler speech of Nov. 8, 1941, in *Der Grossdeutsche Freiheitskampf*, ed. Bouhler, 3, p. 101.

47. See Hitler's comments to Matsuoka Yosuke, Apr. 4, 1941, *Documents on German Foreign Policy, 1918-1945*, Ser. D, XII, No. 266.

48. The former German ambassador to the United States, Hans Heinrich Dieckhoff, tried unsuccessfully to counter this line of argument. (Ibid., 11, No. 633.) Bötticher's views, especially on lend-lease, were again more like Hitler's. (Ibid., 12, Nos. 88, 148, 212.)

49. Trefousse, *Germany and American Neutrality*, p. 155.

50. Ernst von Weizsäcker, *Erinnerungen* (Munich: Paul List, 1950), p. 328.

America unchanged. One month after Pearl Harbor he said: "I'll never believe that an American can fight like a hero."[51] He expressed his "feelings of hatred and deep repugnance" for Americanism and added: "I don't see much future for the Americans. In my view it's a decayed country."[52] That America's entrance into the war might seriously affect its outcome does not seem to have occurred to him. On the contrary, he was overjoyed at Japan's advances in the Pacific and the continued successes of his U-boats in the Atlantic. He was certainly not worried about American leadership: one could become colonel more easily in the American than lieutenant in the German Army;[53] while America's civilian leaders were a group of "nitwits" (*Strohköpfe*).[54] Occasionally Hitler gave vent to his deep hatred of Roosevelt;[55] but convinced of America's inherent inferiority, he refused to be daunted by the prospect of massive American participation. The productivity of American industry—once the object of his envious admiration—was now proclaimed a figment of Roosevelt's imagination.[56]

The first major clash between American and German troops took place in Tunisia in February 1943. In an engagement near Kasserine Pass, the Americans initially suffered reverses; justly or unjustly, two American generals were dismissed for the army's failure to do as well as had been hoped. This episode naturally confirmed Hitler's conviction that the GI was no match for his own battle-hardened veterans.[57] The ultimate defeat of the Germans in

51. *Hitler's Table Talk,* ed. Trevor-Roper, p. 181 (Jan. 5, 1942); cf. *Hitlers Tischgespräche,* ed. Ritter, p. 112 (July 21, 1942).

52. *Hitler's Table Talk,* ed. Trevor-Roper, p. 188 (Jan. 7, 1942).

53. *Hitlers Tischgespräche,* ed. Ritter, p. 385 (Mar. 25, 1942).

54. Ibid., p. 87 (May 17, 1942).

55. Albert Zoller, *Hitler privat, Erlebnisbericht seiner Geheimsekretärin* (Düsseldorf: Droste, 1949), p. 158.

56. *Hitlers Tischgespräche,* ed. Ritter, p. 163 (July 2, 1942). The diary of Goebbels contains many references of this kind.

57. Hitler conference of Mar. 3, 1943, in *Hitler Directs His War, The Secret Records of His Daily Military Conferences,* ed. Felix Gilbert (New

Tunisia led to no revision in Hitler's evaluation. He similarly discounted the impact of American aid to its Allies.[58]

The Sicilian and Italian campaigns of 1943 brought no change in Hitler's views. Looking forward to a possible Allied invasion of Western Europe, Hitler was certain that the American troops "are not qualified to solve this problem. They can't do it. If they had troops with two years' combat experience, one would say they might do it, but they are all new outfits."[59] The Normandy invasion would have convinced any normal person that there was something wrong with the image of a weak America, unable to defend itself, incapable of mobilizing production, and unskilled in military affairs. The simultaneous rapid progress of American operations in the Pacific—the offensives on Biak and Saipan were mounted at about the same time as the Normandy invasion—might also have impressed a thinking observer. But Hitler was hardly a normal person, and reality was no longer allowed to intrude upon his world of dreams and illusions. As Germany's military situation deteriorated, he closed his eyes and ears to new impressions. He would no longer visit the front. He refused to look at Germany's cities as they sank into rubble and dust. He literally buried himself in his East Prussian bunker, where he alternated between interfering in the minutiae of military affairs and pontificating on the nature of the universe.

Germany's desperate exertions enabled it to survive the defeats of the summer and fall of 1944. Its last reserves would make possible one more blow. Hitler decided that nothing much could be accomplished on the Eastern front, but the situation in the West looked different to him.

York: Oxford University Press, 1950), p. 24; *Hitlers Lagebesprechungen*, ed. Heiber, pp. 170-71; *Kriegstagebuch des Oberkommandos der Wehrmacht 1940-1945, 3, 1943*, ed. Walther Hubatsch (Frankfurt a.M.: Bernard & Graefe, 1963), p. 1512.

58. Hitler conference of Dec. 20, 1943 (?), *Hitlers Lagebesprechungen*, ed. Heiber, pp. 433-44. In the same conference, Hitler expressed grave doubts about America's ability to finance its war effort. (Ibid., p. 450.)

59. Ibid., p. 452; *Hitler Directs His War*, ed. Gilbert, p. 80.

There he thought himself confronted by the far weaker and more easily discouraged American and British forces. A successful blow at them might yet bring about a drastic change in the situation. What a land victory in the West had not accomplished in 1940 might still be attained. Thus Germany's last reserves were thrown into the Ardennes offensive, the Battle of the Bulge,[60] and a subsequent smaller offensive, only to be halted by the Americans and soon after shifted to the East to meet the Soviet winter offensive. If nothing else, this last attack in the West shows how persistently Hitler held to his negative evaluation of the United States. It is only fair to add that these views were long shared and reinforced by many of his top-level military advisers.[61] Certainly the vast quantity of German military records made available since the war contains few signs of real awareness of American military potential outside the purely industrial one. The published volumes of the war diary of the German high command's operations staff are most eloquent on this subject by their very silence, in almost two thousand pages for the years 1944-1945.[62]

In the last months of the war, Hitler's mind became increasingly clouded. How far his thoughts had strayed from the realm of reality is illustrated by his reaction to the news of Roosevelt's death. Totally ignorant of the facts of American life, he and his associates neither knew nor cared about the realities of the American system of succession. All they could think of was the death of the Russian Empress Elizabeth in 1762 that had saved Frederick the Great from defeat and Prussia from disaster at the last moment in the

60. Forrest C. Pogue, *The Supreme Command* (Washington, D.C.: Government Printing Office, 1954), Chap. 20; for a contemporary perspective, see Semmler, *Goebbels*, p. 168.

61. Kordt, *Wahn und Wirklichkeit*, p. 142; comments by Alfred Jodl and others at the conference of Mar. 3, 1943, cited in note 57, above; see also the comments on the illusions of Germany's military leaders about American power being tied up in the Far East in the *Kriegstagebuch des Oberkommandos der Wehrmacht 1940-1945*, 3, ed. Hubatsch, pp. 1512-13.

62. *Kriegstagebuch des Oberkommandos der Wehrmacht 1940-1945*, 4, *1944-45*, ed. Percy E. Schramm (Frankfurt, a.M.: Bernard & Graefe, 1961).

Seven Years' War. Here, they thought, was another such miracle—and there was no one to point out that it was a mirage.[63]

Hitler's beliefs had once demonstrated clearly that the United States was racially strong and a dangerous threat. Soon after, these same murky doctrines had revealed to him with equal clarity that the United States was weak and degenerate. These contradictory visions assailed him simultaneously in the last weeks of the war. On the one hand, faced by the streams of American bombers over Germany, he reverted to his earlier recognition of the potential of American industrial might.[64] He now asserted that it was the danger of this war potential looming in the distance that had made an early attack on Russia necessary,[65] and concluded that his war against the United States was a tragedy.[66] On the other hand, he insisted that the United States was an artificial society without soul, culture, or civilization[67] and maintained that "the fact that they [the Americans] combine the possession of such vast material power with so vast a lack of intelligence evokes the image of some child stricken with elephantiasis"; from which in turn he concluded that the United States was "a giant with feet of clay."[68] Even his evaluation of the German-Americans now swung between such extremes. Though they had allegedly lost their souls, these Germans were at one moment described as "the backbone of the country," retaining their characteristics of industry and hard work. Minutes later Hitler explained: "Transplant a German to Kiev, and he remains a perfect German. But transplant him to

63. Semmler, *Goebbels*, pp. 190-93.

64. Hitler conference of Jan. 10, 1945, *Hitlers Lagebesprechungen*, ed. Heiber, pp. 814-15.

65. *The Testament of Adolf Hitler, The Hitler-Bormann Documents, February-April 1945*, ed. François Genoud (London: Cassell, 1961), p. 64 (Feb. 15, 1945).

66. Ibid., p. 87 (Feb. 21, 1945).

67. Ibid., p. 43 (Feb. 7, 1945).

68. Ibid., p. 108 (Apr. 2, 1945).

Miami, and you make a degenerate of him—in other words, an American."[69] Only the total domination of American policy by Jews remained a constant factor in his visions.

In those last macabre days in the Berlin bunker, Hitler could not make up his mind which of the two images of America was right. We might conclude that the reason for this was that both were wrong, but that would involve substituting our standard of truth for his. By his standards—to which he clung as long as he lived—they were both right even though contradictory.

In a totalitarian state, such standards and images become the framework for policy formulation by the dictator. Since the negative assessment of American strength predominated in the years when Hitler was in a position to initiate events, and was supported rather than contradicted by a majority of his advisers, the underestimation of the United States can be seen to have reduced German caution in the 1930's and distorted German military estimates in the 1940's.

Hitler had wanted to divide Germany; he left it divided, though not the way he had intended. He had planned on three wars; he had them, all rolled into one, but they did not come out as he anticipated. The doctrines by which he lived and fought deceived him in death as in life. He committed suicide lest he be captured by the Russians; his last will ended up on display in the United States National Archives.

69. Ibid., pp. 45-46 (Feb. 7, 1945).

Germany's Declaration of War on the United States: A New Look

The decision of the German government to declare war on the United States in December 1941 has puzzled some scholars. The decision was made by Hitler personally, but anticipated as likely by German Foreign Minister von Ribbentrop, greeted with relief—even joy—by the German navy, and as far as is known *not* advised against by a single figure in the German government.[1] It is thus quite unique among German decisions to start or dramatically expand the war. This unusual unanimity on a decision many have often seen as suicidal, or at least stupid, offers room for a reexamination. This reexamination will focus on the perceptions of those who made or knew of the choices between peace and war, perceptions into which war with the United States fitted considerably more easily than the literature on the subject might otherwise lead one to expect.

Hitler himself had begun with an image of a strong United States, an image compounded from the supposed racial advantages of selective immigration and the eco-

The author's work on this topic has been assisted by the National Endowment for the Humanities and the Bellagio Study and Conference Center of the Rockefeller Foundation. It is also published in the *Brooklyn College Studies on Society in Change*, No. 21: *Germany and America: Essays on Problems of International Relations and Immigration*, ed. Hans L. Trefousse (Brooklyn: Brooklyn College Press, 1980), pp. 54-70, and is reprinted here by permission of Brooklyn College of the City University of New York.

1. Note that even State Secretary Ernst von Weizsäcker, who had argued strongly against the German attack on the Soviet Union, took a resigned and largely positive attitude toward war with the United States; see *Die Weizsäcker-Papiere, 1933-1950*, ed. Leonidas E. Hill (Frankfurt am Main: Propyläen, 1974), pp. 278-80.

nomic potential of a huge domestic market. Under the impact of the depression, Hitler had reassessed the racial development of America. He combined his negative view of a racial melting pot, in which the scum naturally floated to the top, with his antipathy for American cultural influences as these were reflected in the developments of Weimar Germany that he most detested; the result was a view of the United States which would remain constant until his suicide.[2] This was a perception of the United States which combined the potential of strength and danger with the actuality of weakness and disarray. The industrial potential of a large country might someday be troublesome for Germany's effort at world domination, but the internal divisions of the country and the incompetence of its leadership assured German triumph. In the long run Germany would have to fight the United States, and it was therefore necessary to inaugurate early appropriate measures in the field of naval construction, since these required the longest lead time for completion.[3] There was, however, no need for great concern in the interim because the weakness of the disarmed and depressed United States precluded any serious American steps that might interfere with Germany's initial foreign policy adventures.

In the years before the war, therefore, Hitler moved without much interest in or concern for American reactions, and with the exception of Fritz Wiedemann, his military adjutant, no one in the higher levels of the German government suggested otherwise to him.[4] As Hans Luther had been elegantly removed from the presidency

2. See the preceding article, "Hitler's Image of the United States."

3. This point is particularly intelligently explained by Jost Dülffer in his book, *Weimar, Hitler und die Marine: Reichspolitik und Flottenbau 1920 bis 1939* (Düsseldorf: Droste, 1973).

4. The one other minor episode, in which Hermann Göring and Franz Pfeffer von Salomon tried to solve the sabotage claims controversy in a manner designed to improve German-American relations in general, is treated in my book, *The Foreign Policy of Hitler's Germany: Diplomatic Revolution in Europe, 1933-36* (Chicago: University of Chicago Press, 1970), pp. 152-54.

of the Reichsbank in 1933 by being shipped off to the insignificant post of Ambassador to the United States, so Wiedemann was exiled to an even less significant—if more scenic—post in San Francisco. Some cautionary dispatches from the German embassy in Washington were easily waved aside, and when the German military attaché to the United States had an opportunity to talk with Hitler in February 1939, the only subject which interested the Fuehrer was the discovery of an alleged Jewish ancestor of President Roosevelt about whom the German government was to launch a great propaganda campaign.[5] The contemptuous dismissal of Roosevelt's peace appeal of April 14, 1939, reflects in both tone and substance the assumption that nothing the United States was likely to do could have a major impact on German plans, which at that time already included a war for that year.

The neutrality policy of the United States undoubtedly reinforced the picture of America held in Berlin. Convinced that entry into World War I had been a terrible mistake, the United States had adopted a policy designed to remove what were perceived to be the causes of that error, regardless of the obvious impossibility of staying out of a war one had entered in 1917. The legislation prohibiting the sale of weapons to belligerents reinforced Germany's headstart in rearmament as Berlin—like London and Paris—well knew, and also prevented the rebuilding of American defense industry with foreign orders. The attempt of President Roosevelt to aid the rebuilding of the French air force crashed quite literally in an incident on January 23, 1939,[6] and the administration's hopes for neutrality law revision failed in a Congress determined to stay out of Kaiser Willie's war. The German government ig-

5. Friedrich von Boetticher, "Soldat am Rande der Politik," Bundesarchiv/Militärarchiv, N 323/56, p. 209.

6. John McVickar Haight, Jr., *American Aid to France, 1938-1940* (New York: Atheneum, 1970), pp. 94-95. An officer attached to the French purchasing mission was aboard a Douglas-DB-7 bomber when it crashed in a demonstration flight. A political uproar ensued.

nored the last minute peace appeals of President Roosevelt and responded to his call for conducting air warfare humanely by dropping a bomb in the garden of the villa Ambassador Biddle had rented as a refuge for the secretaries of the United States legation in Warsaw.

Hitler had hoped to keep his eastern front quiet by the subordination of Poland and Hungary during a war against England and France as the necessary preliminary to the later conquest of European Russia.[7] The refusal of Poland to yield her independence had led him to reverse the sequence. He hoped for war against an isolated Poland but willingly risked a war with France and England since such a war was next on his program in any case. The entrance of the Western Powers into the conflict in September 1939 therefore led to only minor readjustments in German policies. A massive program for the construction of the two-engined Ju-88 dive-bomber would make possible a "deadly blow"[8] at England after an invasion of the Low Countries had enabled the German army to crush France.[9] How did the German government perceive the role of the United States during this stage of the conflict?

The United States was a neutral, and it appeared inclined to provide some help to Germany's enemies. As for the first of these—neutrality—it merely confirmed Hitler's negative assessment of the United States. In his second book he had set forth at considerable length a view that he appears to have adhered to thereafter: neutrality was the policy of the weak, the stupid, and the indecisive, while nations with clear purpose and farsighted leadership took

7. This topic is reviewed in detail in my book, *The Foreign Policy of Hitler's Germany: Starting World War II, 1937-1939* (Chicago: University of Chicago Press, 1980), chap. 12.

8. Göring's report on a conference with Hitler, "Diary of the Chief of Staff of the Allgemeine Heeresamt," September 6, 1939, London, Imperial War Museum, MI 14/981, pp. 132-33.

9. Hitler had explained this aspect of his strategy to his military leaders on May 23, 1939; see *Akten zur deutschen auswärtigen Politik, 1918-1945*, Series D, Vol. VI, p. 481.

advantage of wars started elsewhere either by participating or by starting other wars of their own.[10] Any country not led quite so brilliantly might demonstrate at least a modicum of good sense by assisting one side or the other in return for appropriate concessions, and all who were so inclined were invited to do just that for Germany. The Soviet Union and Spain could both provide secret bases for German naval warfare; Sweden and Japan could provide critically needed raw materials; and any others willing to join the charmed circle of those benevolently neutral to Germany and malevolently neutral to her enemies could be confident of Berlin's very temporary goodwill. There would even be reciprocity, with Germany prepared to assist the Soviet Union in its blockage of Finland just as the Russians would assist the Germans in their attack on Narvik. While the German government from time to time expatiated on the legal aspects of neutrality, such rules were always assumed to be binding only on those neutrals outside the charmed circle.

As for the American inclination to assist Germany's enemies in the war, the German government naturally thought this as evil as it held Soviet aid to itself wise. Hoping to keep his future war with the United States separate from his current war with Poland and the Western Powers, however, Hitler would not heed those of his advisers who were already prepared to risk war with the United States in 1939 and who would continue to urge steps in that direction ever more insistently thereafter: the leaders of the German navy. Since World War II was to see a rerun of sorts of the World War I German internal dispute over unrestricted submarine warfare, a word needs to be said about this issue as seen by the German navy and by Hitler when it first came up in the fall of 1939.[11]

10. See, esp., Gerhard L. Weinberg (ed.), *Hitlers zweites Buch* (Stuttgart: Deutsche Verlags-Anstalt, 1961), chap. 10.

11. These arguments are the subject of an extensive literature. The most important source, the records of Hitler's meetings with Raeder, is

In the eyes of the German naval leadership, the war against England had begun too early. Their own naval construction program was not far enough advanced—the construction programs of others were generally ignored in these calculations. Accordingly Germany would have to make the most of whatever she did have. With England perceived as the main enemy, the navy had since 1918 looked to the war against Britain's transatlantic shipping as the main target of German arms. The very inadequacy of the available means at sea seemed to make it all the more important to use the surface ships and submarines Germany did have without restrictions and cautions. Whatever floated and wherever it went, it should be sent to the bottom as quickly as possible. All else ought to be subordinated to this concept since Germany had no possible alternative strategy for victory over its major foe. This view, eloquently and continuously advanced by Admiral Raeder, was occasionally countered by former Ambassador to the United States Hans Heinrich Dieckhoff, but on the whole met *no* objections from *other* German military and diplomatic figures at the highest levels of the Third Reich.

Hitler himself, however, was by no means certain that the portion of the navy's program likely to bring the United States into the war was, at this early stage of the war, either necessary or wise. What was the point of alarming the United States and stimulating it toward rearmament if a slow tightening of the naval blockade of England would accomplish most of what Germany's small fleet could do anyway? Japan was still an uncertain entity; having been affronted by the German pact with Russia she might relieve the United States of worry in the Pacific and enable her to concentrate on the Atlantic. If Japan and Russia could be reconciled this might change; but in

---

available in a German edition prepared by Gerhard Wagner, *Lagevorträge des Oberbefehlshabers der Kriegsmarine vor Hitler, 1939-1945* (Munich: J. F. Lehmann, 1972).

the meantime why take steps that would alarm American opinion and strengthen Roosevelt's hand at home, but lead only to a minimal increase in sinkings? So each time Raeder came with a request for new measures in the naval war, Hitler allowed some but not all of what had been asked. And as long as the war simmered quietly in the winter of 1939-40, this procedure appeared to serve Germany's purposes.

Hitler, of course, did not intend for the war to simmer quietly forever. The longer an offensive in the West was postponed, the more time his enemies would have to perfect their armaments. Eventually they might even draw on the productive capacity of the United States.[12] The sooner Germany moved the better, and it was primarily bad weather that forced repeated postponements of the attack from November 1939 to May 1940.

That attack appeared at first to accomplish its purpose. France was crushed; Britain was driven off the continent; and the new air and naval bases acquired on the coast facing England and the Atlantic seemed to guarantee the defeat of England. Slow thinkers that they were, the English might take a few weeks to recognize the new reality, but in the meantime Germany could look ahead to the campaigns that would *follow* England's acceptance of the German victory. It is in the plans and projects of June and July 1940 for the direction of German efforts *after* the end of war in Western Europe that we can see more precisely how Hitler and his immediate advisers intended to handle German policy toward the United States.

Once again the critical element would be time. The outbreak of general as opposed to local war in September 1939 had forced a halt on those construction projects of the German navy that looked to the great blue-water fleet. Work had been stopped on all battleships on the schedule

12. This is the clear implication of Hitler's comments on November 23, 1939, see *Akten*, Series D, Vol. 8, p. 347.

beyond the *Tirpitz* as well as on the whole aircraft carrier program. Now that France and England had been defeated, those time- and material-consuming projects could be resumed. It seems to me a key indication of German plans that the immediate intention following the assumption of victory in the West was to reduce the German army and to return to a huge program of battleship construction.[13] No doubt a school of revisionist historians will seek to prove that this was only Hitler's way of coping with the threat Liechtenstein posed for the Third Reich, but it is more likely that Hitler and his advisers were looking not up the Rhine but across the Atlantic.

This interpretation is supported by the simultaneous development of plans for the bases at which the huge new fleet would be stationed, serviced, and if necessary repaired. To the previously projected great new base at Trondheim on the Norwegian coast were now added not only bases on the northern and western coasts of France but also a whole string of bases on and off the coast of northwest Africa. It is worth noting as a sign of the priority which Hitler, in full agreement with his naval advisers, placed on these bases, that when he was confident of victory in Western Europe he was prepared to sacrifice to this concept the participation of Spain in the war on Germany's side.[14] As long as he was sure that England was already beaten, he did not need Spain for that any more; what he needed was bases in French and Spanish Morocco and on the Spanish islands off the African coast for the fleet required by his future policy toward the Western Hemisphere.

13. The reorientation of German armaments planning in the summer of 1940 was first reviewed in some detail in chapters 6 and 7 of my book *Germany and the Soviet Union, 1939-1941* (Leyden: Brill, 1954, 1971); it has been reviewed most recently in Andreas Hillgruber, *Hitlers Strategie: Politik und Kriegführung 1940-1941;* his interpretation is not, however, followed here.

14. My account of this in the following essay, "German Colonial Plans and Policies, 1938-1942," (pp. 112-24), will be replaced by a more detailed analysis in a forthcoming book on World War II.

All these glorious prospects suffered sharp modification as the war Hitler thought concluded failed to end. British determination to continue the war puzzled and angered him. The anger could be relieved by ordering devastating air raids and gearing up for an invasion of the United Kingdom. The puzzle of why the English kept fighting bothered him for some weeks and greatly influenced the decision of late July 1940 to attack the Soviet Union.

A war with the United States had long formed a part of Hitler's conception of Germany's role in the world, and a war with the Soviet Union had always been a portion of his concept of expanding Germany's living space eastward. The question of timing and circumstance had been left open, and if the timing of the decision to attack Russia is no longer in serious dispute, the circumstances are surely worth noting. In the circumstances of the time, an invasion of Russia and the conquest of most or all of its European territory looked to Hitler and most of his military advisers an easier operation than an invasion of England. If the Russian operation was to take place sooner or later anyway, this seemed like a particularly auspicious moment. If launched immediately—and we must recall that Hitler originally hoped to strike in the fall of 1940—there would be great side benefits for the war against England. That country, having lost her major continental ally, must be continuing in the expectation of finding substitutes for France, and for such a role the Soviet Union and the United States were the obvious candidates. An attack on the Soviet Union and its removal as a hope for Britain was not only easier than an attack on the United States, given the readier accessibility of Russia to German military power, but Germany's anticipated success against the Soviet Union would have the further effect of immobilizing the United States as a possible supporter of England as well. The destruction of Soviet military power would free Japan to move forward in Southeast Asia, and thereby pull the attention, energy, and resources of the United States away from the Atlantic and leave Britain without hope of support from anywhere.[15]

To be sure, the decision to attack Russia once again meant a change in German armaments policy. Now the army had to be made bigger, not smaller. The plans for super-battleships had to go back into the files; but submarines could be built quickly to cope with the English, while the Americans would be first diverted to the Pacific by an unleashed Japan and their subsequent fate postponed until the release of German resources *after* the quick defeat of Russia allowed a return to oceanic adventures.[16]

The apparently necessary postponement of an attack on Russia until the spring of 1941 meant that a slow but steady increase in American aid to Britain ran parallel to the equally steady increase of Soviet shipments of supplies to Germany. Berlin frowned on the one as it smiled on the other; it was not easy, however, to decide what to do other than frown. Various German efforts to influence American opinion during and after the 1940 election proved ineffective. The hope that the Tripartite Pact with Japan might spur Tokyo to a more adventurous course was only partially realized, while the United States was alerted rather than deterred by this more formal association of Berlin and Tokyo. The German navy as usual had its answer at hand—sink anything that floated. Hitler still favored a process of limited increments in naval action: increments to reduce the flow of supplies to England, but limits in order

15. Hitler's comments on July 31, 1940 in the diary of Franz Halder are quoted in my book, *Germany and the Soviet Union,* p. 115. Hitler repeated this line of argument to von Bock on December 3, 1940 ("Diary of von Bock," Bundesarchiv/Militärarchiv, N 22/7, f. 2), and to a meeting of military leaders on January 9, 1941 (*Kriegstagebuch des Oberkommandos der Wehrmacht, 1940-1945,* 1 (Frankfurt am Main: Bernard & Graefe, 1964), 257-58.

16. Note Göring's dismissal of a warning about American military potential on August 30, 1940, Munich, Institut für Zeitgeschichte, ZS 115, p. 4.

to postpone a clash with the United States at a time when the German armaments effort had just been directed toward a major increase in land power at the expense of the massive naval program needed to cope with the United States. A study of the effects of a German surprise attack by U-boats on the United States navy while at anchor in its bases which Hitler had ordered—a sort of underwater Pearl Harbor concept—proved insufficiently encouraging;[17] and his projects for seizing the Azores and other islands in the Atlantic to use as bases for bombers to attack American cities were far short of realization.[18] In the interim, that is until Germany could turn her military power directly against the United States, the indirect approach would have to do.

Even before the German attack on Russia opened the road south for Japan, therefore, the Germans tried very hard to encourage the Japanese to move in that direction. The German navy in particular was concerned about Tokyo's delays and constantly urged an attack on Singapore.[19] Raeder's advice to Hitler that Japanese Foreign Minister Matsuoka Yosuke be told of the forthcoming attack on Russia during his visit to Germany in March and April 1941 belongs in this context: if the Japanese knew that the Soviet Union would soon be attacked by Germany, they would be less reluctant to move in the direction Germany wanted, against Singapore.[20] Although Hitler very much

17. Kriegstagebuch der Seekriegsleitung, March 22, 1941, Teil A, Bd. 19, Bundesarchiv/Militärarchiv, RM 7/22, p. 309. The study concluded that anti-submarine nets and other defenses would make it too difficult for U-boats to sneak into American naval bases and anchorages unnoticed.

18. Holger H. Herwig, *Politics of Frustration: The United States in German Naval Planning, 1889-1941* (Boston: Little, Brown, 1976), pp. 214-15, 223. For a thoughtful warning about the possible dangers for Germany in the air rearmament of the United States, see Fritz Siebel to Ernst Udet, October 7, 1940, Imperial War Museum, Milch Papers, Vol. 56, pp. 2926-33.

19. See the entries in the war diary of the Seekriegsleitung for February 22, and April 10, 1941.

20. Ibid., March 3, 1941.

shared Raeder's hope, he would not share his secret. While placing priority on a Japanese attack against Britain's Asian colonies, he reassured Matsuoka about any complications with the United States. If a Japanese move in Southeast Asia, or anywhere else, did lead to war with America, Germany would side with Japan.[21] Whatever his preference for postponing war with the United States, Hitler was quite willing to take part in such a war earlier if that was what was needed to involve Japan in war against England. Hitler never read the Tripartite Pact as narrowly as some of its postwar American interpreters. Quite the contrary, having tried to turn the Japanese against the Western Powers since 1938, he was happy to give the pact the broadest and most aggressive interpretation.

The Japanese government as a whole did not share the German hurry. Its assessment of the risks induced greater caution among at least some elements in Tokyo. Even the non-aggression pact with Russia that Matsuoka signed in Moscow on his return trip failed to remove all the worries in the Japanese capital. The idea of an attack on the exposed colonial possessions of France, Great Britain, and the Netherlands in Southeast Asia looked so inviting as to be almost irresistible, but what about the United States? Guam, tiny, undefended, and indefensible, could be ignored, but the Philippines could not. The Americans would leave in 1946, and it is hardly a coincidence that the Japanese during 1941 repeatedly cited that year to the Germans as the one in which they would be ready to move.[22] Even if the Germans had not pointed it out to them, however, the Japanese knew perfectly well that by then the European war was likely to be over, and that whatever the

21. Hitler's statement to Matsuoka on April 4, 1941 is in *Akten,* Series D, Vol. 12, p. 376.

22. Entries in the war diary of the Seekriegsleitung for April 10 & 21, and May 13, 1941. The Philippines were supposed to receive their independence in 1944, but the law provided for American bases in the islands for an additional two years.

outcome, the United States would be able to devote full attention to Southeast Asia. If Germany won, would it allow Japan to reap the colonial harvest made available by the exertions of German might? If Germany lost, would not the owners of the lands Japan coveted recover their strength? If there were a compromise peace, could Japan risk starting a new war? Surely the time to move—if ever—was now.

These puzzles, and the internal rifts over alternative policies in Tokyo, led to the long exploration of a possible accommodation by Japan with the United States. The aspect of the Japanese-American negotiations of 1941 which needs to be examined here is the relationship of these negotiations to Germany's policy toward the two powers Japan and the United States, one a half-ally, the other a half-enemy. Berlin observed the talks with extreme anxiety. Unlike the Americans, they could not read the main Japanese diplomatic code; by this time they were having much less luck than earlier with the American codes; and the Japanese told the Germans very little. The suspicions of the Germans were quickly, and not unjustifiably, aroused. Twice before, in the summer of 1938 and in the winter of 1938-39, they had failed to secure a firm Japanese commitment against the Western Powers. Now that they were at war, the Germans were not getting from Japan the sort of economic or naval aid they wanted—a particularly galling situation when Berlin compared what Japan was doing for its Tripartite Pact partner with what America was doing for Britain.[23] And now it looked as if the Japanese might reach a real accommodation with the United States which would have the double effect of lessening the chances of a Japanese attack on Britain and relieving American concern in the Pacific. The obverse of an unleashed Japan drawing the United States into the Pacific was obviously a qui-

23. Ibid., April 17, and May 23, 1941.

escent Japan allowing the United States to increase its support of Britain in the Atlantic.[24]

The anxiety of the Germans was raised to a very high level by almost simultaneous developments during May of 1941. On the one hand, there appeared to be a real chance of progress in the United States-Japanese negotiations. The Japanese refusal at one point to oblige the Germans by waiting for a few days for German observations on a new proposal in early May led the German authorities to suspect the worst. In repeated conferences, Hitler and von Ribbentrop reviewed the situation.[25] But they could only wave frantically from the sidelines, warning Japan of American perfidy, and emphasizing the golden opportunity of the moment. Soon after, the sinking of the *Bismarck* struck a major blow at German hopes in the Battle of the Atlantic. The approaching deadline for the attack on Russia reinforced Hitler's concern about the defense of Norway and combined with British bombing of Brest to produce Hitler's decision to station the remaining large German surface ships in Norwegian waters. Although this resolve was not finally implemented by a reluctant navy until February 1942, Hitler's thinking, as Raeder well knew, had been moving in this direction long before. Combined with other naval losses and the sinking of the *Bismarck,* this trend effectively dashed all remaining hopes about a resumption of surface raiding by German fleet units in the Atlantic. The obvious deduction was that the increasing stream of American supplies to England should be cut by the submarines.

Believing that the United States was doing as much as it could under any circumstances, the naval leaders could see little sense in avoiding formal American entrance into the war. Although Hitler shared the assessment of America's limited potential in spite of contrary advice from former

24. Ibid., June 13, 1941.

25. Note the entry for May 8, 1941 in the Hewel Diary, Munich, Institut für Zeitgeschichte.

Ambassador Dieckhoff,[26] he still preferred to postpone formal American participation. In his eyes a quick triumph over Russia might, as he had calculated originally, end the war for the time being—thus giving him time to build a real surface navy—by depriving England of all her potential allies. With Russia eliminated, the Japanese would surely keep America preoccupied, and until 1942 the United States would not be able to do much in any case. The days just before and after the invasion of Russia were therefore a time to avoid incidents in the Atlantic.[27]

The first weeks of the attack on Russia gave many leaders of the Third Reich the impression that the campaign would soon be over. Accordingly they began promptly with plans for the period *after* victory in the East had been attained. Of these, some were extensions of the eastern campaign itself; for example, the expansion of the program to murder the Jews of occupied Russia to include those of all of Europe, and the projects for using the newly occupied areas as bases for an assault on the British position in the Near East. Our interest must focus on the project pointing in the opposite direction. In the late summer of *1940* the projected blue-water fleet had been pushed aside by the higher immediate priority of the planned campaign against Russia. In July *1941,* however, as in June and July of 1940, German "postwar planning" once again included the huge surface fleet. Projected at 25 battleships, 8 aircraft carriers, 50 cruisers, 400 submarines, 150 destroyers, and miscellaneous other ships,[28] it provides important insight into German long-term policy aims toward the

26. On Dieckhoff's views, see *Akten,* D, 11, No. 633; for his comments on the silly reports of the German military attaché von Boetticher, see *Akten,* 12, No. 600. Von Boetticher's reports are summarized in James V. Compton, *The Swastika and the Eagle* (Boston: Houghton Mifflin, 1967), chap. 7, and should be contrasted with his memoirs in the Bundesarchiv/Militärarchiv.

27. Entry for May 22, 1941 in Hewel Diary (see n. 25). Hitler's comments of June 14, 1941 are in Franz Halder, *Tagebuch,* 2: 455.

28. "Skl IIIa 17233/g.Kdos.," July 31, 1941, Bundesarchiv/Militärarchiv, RM 6/83, ff. 49-50.

Western Hemisphere—unless one is prepared to assume that the big ships were to be sent down the Danube or hauled by rail to the Caspian Sea.

As the fighting in the East continued, the program for murdering Jews went forward and that for attacking the Near East had to be postponed a year, but the plan to re-order priorities in the armaments field to the navy once again evaporated. For a moment it looked as if as a substitute Japan might be lured into the war by the backdoor of having her join in crushing Russia, but that project was soon abandoned, at least by Hitler.[29] The fact that the United States was helping Russia as well as Britain, however, suggested other perspectives: how much more than helping England and Russia could America do? and if very little, then why spare her ships and shipping lanes?[30]

On the other side of the globe, the Japanese were now relieved of the danger they felt at their own backdoor. Japan's main concern now was what they saw, quite correctly, as a British-American strategy of stalling for time in East Asia while defeating Germany and then confronting Japan with overwhelming power in the Pacific.[31] Having had their own very sad experiences with the Red Army in 1938 and 1939, the Japanese expected the survival of the Soviet Union and the likelihood of a new German-Soviet accommodation rather than a collapse of Russia, so that the developments on the Eastern Front suggested to them that the time for Japan to move South might well be at hand.[32] And this was certainly what they heard from the Germans.[33]

When the Japanese decided to go forward they did so in a context of assuming that Germany and Italy would be their allies while the Soviet Union would remain neutral. Their own attack would be directed against the United

29. See Andreas Hillgruber, *Deutsche Grossmacht- und Weltpolitik im 19. und 20. Jahrhundert* (Düsseldorf: Droste, 1977), pp. 230-31.

30. Note the Seekriegsleitung war diary for August 13, 1941.

31. Ibid., Sept. 27, 1941.

32. Ibid., Oct. 4, 1941.

33. Ibid., Oct. 25, 1941.

States and Great Britain, and they certainly wanted those countries denied bases in the Soviet Far East, a subject on which they sounded the Russians beforehand.[34] Their question to Berlin and Rome as to whether those countries would join them in war on the United States was asked with the thought that if their Tripartite Pact partners responded with a request for a declaration of war on Russia, Japan would decline.[35] What would be the answer from Berlin?

When the Japanese Ambassador to Germany raised this question with von Ribbentrop on November 30, 1941, Hitler was preoccupied with the crisis on the Eastern Front. Von Ribbentrop said that Germany would immediately join in the war with America—he had said about the same thing spontaneously a few days earlier—but he would need Hitler's official approval to make the statement authoritative.[36] Surely von Ribbentrop had discussed the matter with Hitler earlier and was confident in his own mind that he was accurately reflecting his master's views, as we know he had heard Hitler express them to Matsuoka. Hitler's views had indeed remained unchanged, and von Ribbentrop could therefore reassure Oshima Hiroshi on the point early on December 5.[37] The Germans believed Japanese-American relations to be at the breaking point, but we must remember that they did not know Japan intended to strike in a few days—any more than they had known when they gave similar assurances in April that Tokyo would wait for several months.

Why was Hitler, who had been trying to avoid incidents in the Atlantic, willing to go to war now? A series of reasons emerges out of his prior policies. With Great Britain still perceived as a key, if not the key, enemy of Germany,

34. George A. Lensen, *The Strange Neutrality: Soviet-Japanese Relations during the Second World War, 1941-1945* (Tallahassee, Fla.: Diplomatic Press, 1972), pp. 35-38.

35. *Pearl Harbor Attack*, Pt. 12, p. 204.

36. *Akten*, 13, Nos. 537, 546.

37. *Pearl Harbor Attack*, Pt. 35, pp. 684-85.

if this were what it took to get Japan to move against that country, then so be it. Especially if the alternative might be a modus vivendi between Japan and the United States which would release America from concerns in the Pacific and enable it to concentrate on the Atlantic. Instead of greater difficulties in the Atlantic, the alternative of war with the United States offered Germany the hope—daily stressed by Hitler's naval leaders—of massive successes by his U-boats in that very theater. Convinced that Germany had lost World War I because of the "Stab-in-the-back" by a home front beguiled by the promises of President Wilson, he was certain that there could be no repetition: the German public would never fall for such tricks again, and any so inclined would be crushed if still at large. Since Hitler did not believe that American military might, as opposed to its propaganda, had played any significant part in the victory of the Entente over Germany, he saw no reason to fear such might now, or at least during the coming year when he anticipated major victories on the Eastern front. If he was going to have to fight the United States sooner or later anyway—as he had believed for years and as he had so often tried to factor into his armaments program—then this, if not the ideal moment, was assuredly an acceptable time. In 1939 he had made the same calculation in regard to England; though preferring to postpone war in the West and deal only with Poland, he had accepted the likelihood of war with England then rather than later. And now an analogous choice vis-à-vis the United States was before him, not with an Italy dithering on the sidelines as in 1939 but with a Japan prepared to commit herself against Britain and the United States first. The earlier premium on delay was now much smaller.

Since the Japanese were as careful not to reveal their plans to the Germans as the latter had been to conceal their own, the attack on Pearl Harbor came as a most pleasant surprise for Berlin. The idea of a Sunday morning attack in peacetime had been tried out by the Germans themselves on Belgrade earlier that year, and the Japanese imitation evoked nothing but applause. As for the immediately following Japanese question about Germany's participation, that would be answered in the affirmative. Again Hitler had to be asked formally, and since he happened to be away from his regular headquarters to deal with a crisis in command and strategy at the southern end of the Eastern front, there was a short delay in securing an answer; but all speculations about this delay derive from overlooking the practical problems of getting a decision from Hitler at that moment. Hitler himself had no hesitation. His positive views as expressed a few days earlier in response to Oshima's question about Germany's willingness in principle to join a war against America could only be reinforced by what had happened in the meantime. Here was an ally which obviously knew its business, and the sooner all joined together, the better.

Unlike previous occasions when Germany had taken the whole initiative in expanding the war, this time the formal arrangements had to be made after action taken by others elsewhere. It would take a few days to have the propaganda scenery set up in Berlin. Hitler had to get back to the capital, and the Reichstag deputies had to be summoned from all over to acclaim the happy news of war with the United States. December 11 was the earliest practicable day for this martial celebration, but that did not look to Hitler like any reason to postpone fighting the Americans. That could start forthwith. In the night of December 8-9, therefore, he gave the German navy orders to proceed at once with the sinking of American vessels as well as the ships of all those countries that had declared their solidarity with the United States.[38] No one then knew that the English au-

38. The written confirmation is in the Seekriegsleitung war diary for December 9, 1941 (RM 7/31, pp. 135-36). The countries listed were Uruguay, Panama, Costa Rica, Nicaragua, Honduras, Haiti, El Salvador, and the Dominican Republic.

thor David Irving would one day prescribe retroactively how Hitler was supposed to give orders for historians to accept them as having been given, so no one questioned the oral directives of the Fuehrer. Long straining at the leash, the German navy could now pounce upon its prey in the Atlantic. The ceremonies of December 11 confirmed rather than initiated the state of war between Germany and the United States.

There is a final question to be dealt with. Why did not the German leaders ask Japan to go to war with Russia when the Japanese asked the Germans to join them in fighting the United States? This looks like an obvious question, given the troubles the Germans were then having in the East.[39] Hitler saw the issue differently. He knew that Japan's power was not unlimited. Tied up in a long war in China, Japan could not be expected to make a major contribution to fighting Great Britain—his first concern; to take on the United States and divert the full attention of that power to the Pacific; and also to become embroiled in still another land war in Asia. If Germany had wanted Japan to attack Russia, what had been the point of always urging her to employ her resources in an attack on Singapore? Only in the summer of 1941, when it looked as if there might be a Japanese-American agreement, had Hitler asked for a Japanese attack on Russia as a backdoor through which to get the hesitating ally into the fray. Now, when Japan was willing to move on its own, was hardly the time to raise questions that might lead to a total reconsideration of the issue in Tokyo. If the Japanese believed they could attack Great Britain only if they also went to war with the United States, then Germany should make this decision as easy, not as difficult, as possible for them. For years the Japanese had demonstrated to the

39. During the last ten days of November the Germans were not only being slowed down before Moscow but were in serious trouble at Tikhvin and Rostov at the northern and southern ends of the main front in the East.

Germans that they were all too inclined to delay decisions, and Hitler had no desire to stimulate *that* tendency. On the contrary, a prompt and positive response from Berlin might at last assist those in Japan who favored war. Certainly there was no point in assisting the Tokyo peace faction—if any remained—by qualified answers or additional questions. After all, Hitler expected to beat the Russians next year by himself, thought little of the war-making capabilities of the United States, and expected to fight that power at some point in time anyway. Like the policy makers in Washington, those in Germany in December as in April of 1941 were looking primarily at the expected Japanese move south. With Japan apparently poised on the brink, at last ready to join Germany in a war against Great Britain, Germany ought to provide a quick shove, not a new puzzle.

Few Germans were in any position to bring their views on this matter to the attention of the dictator. Unlike all other major policy choices of the regime, however, this was one on which there appear to have been no oral or written dissents. Only rarely during the escalation of incidents in the Atlantic, never during the attempt to involve Japan in war with Great Britain, and certainly not in the final crisis did anyone among Hitler's political, diplomatic, or military leaders advocate a more cautious approach. Many had argued at one point or another against earlier measures to expand the war. Only this one time was the unanimity of the Reichstag mirrored in the apparatus of government. Hope or resignation, stupidity or wilful ignorance elsewhere, for once enabled the Fuehrer to follow his intuition without contrary advice. There is a curious irony in a situation where the leaders of a country were united on war with the one nation they were least likely and worst equipped to defeat.

German Colonial Plans and Policies, 1938-1942

I.

In *Mein Kampf,* as in his second book, Adolf Hitler had condemned the colonial policy of the Second Reich, primarily because it was in fact not a colonial policy at all in the sense that he wished the term used. Colonialism to him meant the acquisition of territories suitable for German settlement after the expulsion, extermination, or enslavement of the local population. Lands suitable for such treatment were, in his opinion, available only in Eastern Europe—those outside Europe having been preempted by others before Germany appeared on the colonial scene. The acquisition of Germany's colonial empire in the last two decades of the nineteenth century had been, in his opinion, merely a facet of German trade policy with harmful effects on Germany's diplomatic position in the world. During the 1920's, the National Socialist Party paid relatively little attention to the continuing agitation by colonial enthusiasts in Germany;[1] but with the seizure of power, the Party inherited the colonial movement in Germany and "coordinated" it, a process that was simplified by the

The author's work on this study was assisted by a grant from the Horace H. Rackham School of Graduate Studies of the University of Michigan. The article originally appeared in *Geschichte und Gegenwartsbewusstsein: Festschrift für Hans Rothfels* (Göttingen: Vandenhoeck & Ruprecht, 1963), pp. 462-91. It is reprinted here by permission of Vandenhoeck & Ruprecht.

1. The survey by Mary E. Townsend, "Hitler and the Revival of German Colonialism," in *Nationalism and Internationalism, Essays Inscribed to Carlton J. H. Hayes,* ed. Edward M. Earle (New York: Columbia University Press, 1950), pp. 399-430, is useful though adding little new information.

strongly rightist character of the members and leaders of the colonial societies.[2] The activities of these organizations in the 1930's, and Hitler's eventual oratorical support for their aims, attracted world-wide publicity in the prewar years. During World War II, the subject almost disappeared from sight;[3] and since the war, as the author has previously stated in discussing German-Japanese negotiations on the South Seas Mandates in 1937-38,[4] few have paid any attention to the matter. The only major work on prewar diplomacy that has taken newly available material into account is Boris Celovsky's fine study of Munich,[5] but there the colonial question is given a one-sided interpretation as Hitler's blackmail to secure British acquiescence in Germany's Central European policy.[6] In fact, in the very years discussed by Celovsky, the ideological reconciliation of a "Lebensraum" policy in Europe and colonial aspirations elsewhere was being worked out. It is presented most succinctly by Hermann Behrens in an article appropriately entitled "Eastern and Colonial Policy—Their Complementary Necessity" in the October, 1937, issue of *Deutscher Kolonial-Dienst.*[7] Behrens, the associate editor

2. Thus the Party inherited the most eminent spokesman of German colonialism, the former governor of German East Africa, Heinrich Schnee. Elected to the Reichstag in 1924 for the German Peoples Party (DVP), he ran in 1933 and thereafter on the NSDAP ticket. He was in reality quickly pushed aside by Ritter von Epp.

3. One of the few exceptions is Fritz T. Epstein's article, "National Socialism and French Colonialism," *Journal of Central European Affairs,* 3 (April, 1943), 52-64.

4. "Deutsch-japanische Verhandlungen über das Südseemandat 1937-1938," *Vierteljahrshefte für Zeitgeschichte,* 4 (1956), 390 f.

5. *Das Münchener Abkommen von 1938* (Quellen und Darstellungen zur Zeitgeschichte 3) (Stuttgart: Deutsche Verlags-Anstalt, 1958), pp. 40 f., 175 f. On the matters discussed there, see also Lord Halifax, *Fulness of Days* (New York: Dodd, Mead, and Co., 1957), p. 189.

6. There is now a detailed study by Klaus Hildebrand, *Vom Reich zum Weltreich: Hitler, NSDAP und koloniale Frage, 1919-1945* (Munich: Wilhelm Fink, 1969). For the prewar period, the colonial issue has been integrated into my volumes on *The Foreign Policy of Hitler's Germany.*

7. Ost- und Kolonialpolitik: ihre ergänzende Notwendigkeit, 2 (1937), No. 10, pp. 1-8.

of this organ of the Nazi Party's Colonial Policy Office, asserted that Germany needed both land for settlement and raw materials in which she was deficient. While Eastern Europe was suitable for settlement, it lacked many of the raw materials Germany required; colonial territories in Africa would provide the raw materials but were unsuitable for settlement. Germany, therefore, obviously had to have both. The propagation of these doctrines on the relationship of territorial aspirations in Europe and Africa in the public eye came to be a major concern of Werner Daitz's Gesellschaft für europäische Wirtschaftsplanung und Grossraumwirtschaft,[8] while the formal indoctrination with colonial ideas was under the supervision of the Party's Colonial Policy Office.[9] But what was the policy of the German government, what were Hitler's plans and hopes? Although no exhaustive reply to these questions can yet be given, important new evidence, combined with previously available but often neglected information, does provide some insight into the evolution of policy on the colonial subject.

II.

In the winter of 1937-38, the German government was seriously concerned with colonial issues for the first time since 1933. This was the time when abortive negotiations took place with the Japanese[10] and the British. The first involvement of the German armed forces in active colonial

8. See the society's Sonderheft, Karl Krüger, *Kolonialanspruch und kontinentale Wirtschaftsplanung* (Dresden: Meinhold, 1940), p. 26; its confidential second activity report, *Forschungen und Erkenntnisse* (Dresden: Meinhold, 1942), p. 24; and its publication, Adolf Ratenieks, *Was bringt die Neuordnung Europas den europäischen Völkern* (Dresden: Meinhold, 1942), passim.

9. See the "Richtlinien für die kolonialpolitische Schulung" in *Deutscher Kolonial-Dienst*, 4 (1939), No. 1, pp. 12-17. For a useful, though obviously biased presentation, see the chapter on Epp's colonial activity in Joseph H. Krumbach, *Franz Ritter von Epp, Ein Leben für Deutschland* (Munich: Eher, 1939).

10. Weinberg, "Südseemandat," pp. 390-98.

preparations began in this period. An officer in the intelligence branch of the High Command of the Armed forces (OKW/Ausl I), Colonel von Geldern-Crispendorf, who was to be a central figure in German colonial plans, was ordered to begin colonial preparations from the overall standpoint of the armed forces, preparing, in cooperation with the army and navy, for the activation of military units to be used in colonial areas.[11] While the Czech crisis kept Geldern (and presumably the High Command of the Army) occupied with other problems during most of 1938,[12] the German navy initiated the activation of a colonial landing force (Stosstrupps) in May of 1938. Two such units, of company strength each, were established; they were stationed at Swinemünde and Cuxhaven, and by the following year were being furnished with equipment for employment in the tropics.[13] Other activities of the military in the spring and summer of 1938 were restricted to such matters as registering members of the armed forces with colonial experience and studying the resources of the former German colonies.[14]

After the German annexation of parts of Czechoslovakia in October 1938, Hitler turned to new objectives. Poland was next on the agenda, but simultaneously he wanted colonial propaganda intensified—though not to a degree obscuring other aims—and preparations pushed forward. Work on this was resumed in the High Command of the Armed forces (OKW).[15] The Foreign Ministry expanded

11. OKW/WWi VI (Reichmann), "Besprechungsnotiz über den Stand der Bearbeitung von Kolonialfragen bei der Wehrmacht und im Reich," Dec. 6, 1938, National Archives Microcopy T-77, Roll 642, frame 1838571.

12. Ibid. (Geldern's papers are now in the Bundesarchiv/Militärarchiv.)

13. Ibid. OKW/Ausl VII, "Bericht 3 über den Stand der kolonialen Vorarbeiten," Apr. 18, 1939, ibid., frame 1838577; OKW/Ausl VII, "Bericht 4 über den Stand der kolonialen Vorabeiten," June 6, 1939, ibid., frame 1838556.

14. OKW/Ausl VII, "Bericht I über den Stand der kolonialen Vorarbeiten," Jan. 27, 1939, ibid., frame 1838563; OKW/WStb, Reichmann to Reuter No. 617/39g of Jan. 24, 1939, ibid., frames 1838565 f.

15. For this and the following, see OKW/WWi VI, "Besprechungsnotiz

its activities through both its regular channels (Section Pol X) and one of Ribbentrop's former associates from the *Dienststelle Ribbentrop,* Rudolf Karlowa, later appointed to the Bureau of the Foreign Minister with the rank of consul general.[16] The Colonial Policy Office of the NSDAP was intensifying its work, and Hitler had apparently already indicated that it would eventually become a colonial ministry (unlike the Party's Foreign Policy Office under Rosenberg which continued its separate existence alongside the Foreign Ministry). The navy had established its first colonial units and appears to have been one of the driving forces behind the colonial preparations. Now that the Czech crisis was over, temporarily at least, the army designated the 69th Infantry Regiment in Hamburg for the first colonial assignment. German activity in the former colonial areas themselves appears to have been stepped up.[17] As to the specific colonies to be demanded, the official line was to insist on the return of all the former colonies, with no compensation scheme like the then much discussed Pirow-Plan to be considered.

In the period December 1938 to February 1939 a number of conferences and discussions were held to define jurisdictions, outline tasks, and delineate organizational responsibilities—the favorite activity of most civilian and military bureaucrats of the Third Reich. On December 20, 1938, Admiral Canaris and Captain Bürkner of the OKW met with Epp, the chief, and with other high officials of the Colonial Policy Office in Munich. It was agreed that the OKW would prepare the troops, the Colonial

über den Stand der Bearbeitung von Kolonialfragen bei der Wehrmacht und im Reich," Dec. 6, 1938, ibid., frames 1838570-572.

16. Karlowa contributed several articles to *Deutscher Kolonial-Dienst* and other periodicals, all dealing with colonial questions, and wrote: *Die wirtschaftliche Seite des deutschen Kolonialproblems* (Stuttgart: Kohlhammer, 1940). Geldern, in the report cited above, referred to him as a "very knowledgeablc expert" (sehr beschlagener Experte).

17. Gerd May to the OKW/Wi Rü Amt/Abt. Rü VI, Aug. 24, 1940, T-77/642/1838495.

Policy Office the police for colonial possessions. Technical arrangements were agreed upon, the Colonial Policy Office acting somewhat under the influence of recent Italian experiences with a militarized colonial administration. On January 10, 1939, the OKW and the Foreign Ministry discussed colonial problems: the Foreign Ministry was initiating negotiations with the Colonial Policy Office for defining their respective responsibilities—a polite description for a jurisdictional fight that was to be settled by Hitler. On January 14, Epp met with the surviving former German colonial governors, and in February the participants of this conference were to attend a conference in the Transportation Ministry with OKW representatives also present. Alongside all this talking, some action was taking place. The training of colonial officers and administrators, and especially doctors and veterinarians in tropical medicine, was either in progress or in preparation. Relevant manuals were being drafted, and the needed mapmaking had been inaugurated.[18]

Although the precise details of policy formulation are as yet unknown, the evidence does show that out of these and other conferences certain lines of policy emerged. Colonel Geldern informed an officer of the War Economy and Armaments Office of the High Command of the Armed Forces on February 6, 1939, of the current status of preparations and policy decisions; the record of their meeting shows (1), the military preparations were still in a very rudimentary state; (2) little attention had as yet been given to the whole economic side; (3) the peaceful occupation would be initiated by the navy, which would relieve the garrisons of the mandatory powers; and (4) Epp intended to develop the acquired colonies very slowly. As for the

18. OKW/Ausl VII, "Bericht I über den Stand der kolonialen Vorarbeiten," Jan. 27, 1939, ibid., frames 1838561-564. There was also a conference at the High Command of the German Navy (1. Skl) on January 27, Marinekommandoamt to 1. Abt. Skl No. 2330/39gKdos of 14 Oct. 1939, ibid., frame 1838549.

German demand for colonies, Geldern voiced the view that the question would not become acute until the summer of 1939 and stated, presumably on the basis of new directives from above, that Germany's demands would first concentrate on recognition of her legal claims; the question of possible compensation (for any then not reclaimed in fact) would be considered after the German right to ownership had been admitted.[19] At a time when the Germans still hoped to bully the Polish government into major concessions without recourse to war, Hitler apparently thought of raising the colonial question with the Western Powers next. In determining policy for this prospect, Hitler clearly emphasized the primarily political side of the question, ignoring the economic aspects that otherwise figured largely in the colonial agitation. Having faced up to the question of how to resume the colonial negotiations broken off early in 1938, Hitler had reversed the anti-compensation view of a few weeks before to return to the more favorable attitude he had expressed to Lord Halifax in November 1937.

The most important jurisdictional question was also settled. On February 13, 1939, Epp met with Hitler who decided that the work of preparing the future colonial administration was to be centralized in the Colonial Policy Office of the Party, not in Ribbentrop's Foreign Ministry. While Minister Lammers was preparing the official formulation of this decision—which will be discussed below—Epp immediately organized an interagency central committee for the German colonies under his own direction. Subordinate to it were to be four special committees for Southwest Africa, German East Africa, Cameroons, and Togo, a clear sign that Hitler must have told Epp to confine himself to

19. "Deutschlands koloniale Forderungen sollen vorläufig auf Rechtsanspruch beschränkt bleiben; Kompensationen erst nach Erfüllung des Rechtsanspruchs vorgesehen." Hauptmann Rentsch (OKW/WiRü Amt), "Aktennotiz, Betr.: Besprechung zwischen Oberst von Geldern-Crispendorf und Hauptmann Dr. Rentsch am 6. 2. 39." ibid., frame 1838559.

planning for African colonies (thus excluding the former German possessions in the Pacific).[20]

After what must have been extensive consideration, Hitler's decisions were officially formulated and communicated in a confidential letter of March 9, 1939, by Lammers to Epp, with copies going to the Foreign Ministry and the High Command of the Armed Forces, which informed the three services.[21] Hitler wished the preparations for the colonial administration centralized in the Colonial Policy Office, while the Foreign Ministry was to retain full control over all steps, necessarily in the diplomatic field, for the actual reacquisition of colonies. Within this allocation of duties, the two were to cooperate closely, with the Party's Colonial Policy Office remaining a Party institution for the time being, not yet transformed into a state Colonial Ministry as suggested by Epp. This transformation and the future colonial administration were, however, to be prepared simultaneously. On the details of the latter, Hitler obviously did not wish to commit himself as yet, though Epp had made extensive written suggestions. On only one point would Hitler specify future policy: he explicitly directed Epp not to take any steps toward the later establishment of black troop units. In prior years, in *Mein Kampf* and in his second book, Hitler had attacked most vehemently the large-scale use of native troops by the French. Accentuated by the German furor over the inclusion of French colonial units in the Rhineland occupation, the denunciation of French colonial troop recruitment had long been—and continued to be—a prominent feature of National Socialist and German colonialist propaganda. On the other hand, the German colonialist literature had always stressed—and with considerable justification—that the black soldiers who had fought for Germany in the

20. OKW/Ausl VII, "Bericht II über den Stand der kolonialen Vorarbeiten," Feb. 24, 1939, ibid., frames 1838557 f.

21. Lammers to Epp, "RM Nr. 747/39 A," March 9, 1939, copy in ibid., frames 1838579 f.

colonies in World War I, the Askaris, had been intensely loyal, militarily effective, and, in a sense, a testimony for native support of German colonial rule. In the glorification of the Askaris this last aspect had played a particularly important part, for it aided the effort to refute the claim of German colonial misdeeds and unfitness that allegedly justified the eviction of Germany from Africa. Here—as in the case of Germany's relations with Japan—racist lunacies conflicted with political aspirations. In this instance, Hitler held to his deeply felt convictions, probably one of the few he ever had; but as will be seen, his decision by no means foreclosed further agitated consideration of the question.

Of more immediate concern to the German government in March of 1939 than the recruitment of black soldiers was the invasion of Czechoslovakia and the occupation of Prague. Although this step was followed by a visible stiffening of British policy and the continued refusal of Poland to submit to Germany, Hitler reaffirmed the foregoing general colonial policy directive in the middle of April.[22] A variety of preliminary preparatory steps were taken during the summer months by the armed forces,[23] but these were primarily occupied by the preparatory steps for the forthcoming German attack on Poland. Having been commissioned with the launching of Germany's new colonial empire, Epp was naturally concerned with far different problems and inclined to view the developing situation from other perspectives. On May 15 he told Geldern that Hitler had no further continental demands after the

22. OKW/Ausl VII, "Bericht 3 über den Stand der kolonialen Vorabeiten," April 18, 1939, ibid., frames 1838577 f.

23. Ibid.; OKW/WStb, Rohstoffabteilung, "Nr. 1776/39g an WWi (VI), Betr. Bereitstellung geeigneter Treibstoffmittel für motorisierte Einheiten in den Kolonien," May 17, 1939, ibid., frame 1838576; OKW/Ausl VII, "Bericht 4 über den Stand der kolonialen Vorarbeiten," June 6, 1939, ibid., frames 1838555 f.; Admiral Raeder's conference of June 28, 1939 referred to in Marinekommandoamt to 1. Abt. Skl 2330/39gKdos of Oct. 14, 1939, ibid., frame 1838549.

settlement of the Danzig question.[24] The colonial issues could, therefore, become acute during the following year. Since military units required considerable retraining and re-equipping before they could be employed in the tropics, Epp expressed the hope that the armed forces would see to it that the necessary steps be taken in time. Whatever the military might do—and we now know that because of other duties they did next to nothing—the Party Treasury, at Hitler's order, had put up half a million marks so that Epp could establish a new training institute for colonial administrators to open in the fall. The Minister of Economics was working on special currency to be used in the colonies, and the Ministry of the Interior was organizing special police units for colonial employment. The Postal Ministry had officials ready for Togo and the Cameroons, while the Transportation Ministry was also hard at work. The prospective postmasters of Lomé and Douala had to wait, however, as Hitler detoured via Warsaw into a world war.

III.

During the first months of World War II, little was said or done on the colonial question. In his Reichstag speech of October 6, 1939, Hitler demanded the return of Germany's colonies; and about the same time circles in the German navy urged that some thought be given to Germany's former territories in New Guinea, Nauru, and nearby islands because of their gold and phosphate resources.[25] Of greater significance for an understanding of German colonial policy is the information to be derived from Germany's attempts at subversion in the Union of

24. Geldern's record does not disclose whether he and Epp were fooled by this assurance, which Hitler might well have given Epp. For this and the following, see OKW/Ausl VII, "Bericht über die Reichskolonialtagung in Wien vom 15. bis 18. Mai 1939," June 6, 1939, ibid., frames 1838551-554.

25. Marinekommandoamt to 1. Abt. Skl 2330/39gKdos of Oct. 14, 1939, ibid., frames 1838549 f.

South Africa. By August of 1942, Heinrich Himmler was toying with such exotic schemes as raising a revolt in South Africa by attaching leaflets to migrating storks,[26] but in the winter of 1939-40 the Germans were engaged in a more prosaic effort to capitalize on the anti-British and pro-Nazi sympathies of the extreme Afrikaner nationalists led by Daniel Malan and General Hertzog. Only fragmentary evidence on these maneuvers has come to light. With Consul General Karlowa handling the details in Berlin, a special emissary was sent to South Africa; the emissary's wife met Malan in Capetown on January 16, 1940.[27] The aspect of these shadowy activities relevant here is the handling of the question of former German Southwest Africa in the Ribbentrop-approved policy statement transmitted to Malan. Germany insisted that she would reclaim her old African empire, including Southwest Africa. To compensate a Nationalist South African government for this territory, Germany would see to it that the Union received the long—and still—coveted protectorates of Swaziland, Bechuanaland, and Basutoland from England, and Germany further indicated acquiescence if South Africa annexed Southern Rhodesia.[28] The soundings undertaken two years earlier for a possible sale of Germany's claim in Southwest Africa to the Union[29] thus had given way to a renewed determination for recovery of the area: if it was

26. Himmler Files, Drawer 1, Folder 22.

27. Trompke to Ribbentrop, Jan. 26, 1940, *Documents on German Foreign Policy, 1918-1945*, Series D (hereafter referred to as *German Documents D*), Vol. 8 (Washington, D.C.: Government Printing Office, 1954), No. 577; Memorandum of Karlowa, Feb. 22, 1940, ibid., No. 629; Note by Karlowa, March 29, 1940, ibid., Vol. 9 (Washington, D.C.: Government Printing Office, 1956), No. 25. See also Memorandum of Bielfeld, Oct. 8, 1940, *German Documents D*, Vol. 11 (Washington, D.C.: Government Printing Office, 1960), No. 163.

28. Did this imply the possibility that Germany wanted *Northern* Rhodesia for herself to join German Southwest to German East Africa? This was included in at least one German plan; see note 91. (The old colonial names are used in the text since it was in terms of their borders that all discussions took place.)

29. Weinberg, "Südseemandat," p. 392, n. 8.

to be taken from a friendly Nationalist government, it would certainly not be left to a Union that had fought Germany to the end.

The campaign in the West naturally absorbed German attention in the spring of 1940. The successful attack on Holland and Belgium, however, had potential implications of great importance in the colonial field. Dutch Guiana and the Dutch West Indies were out of reach—military inaccessibility combined with the diplomatic dangers of involvement with the United States. The Dutch East Indies were, at that time, even farther removed from the reach of German military power, but of greater significance was the fact that this rich area was a most tempting and eagerly sought after prize for Japan. The Germans on May 20, 1940, expressed to the Japanese government their "disinterestedness" in the Netherlands East Indies,[30] and no evidence has yet turned up to indicate that the Germans ever gave any thought to carving out colonial advantages for themselves in this area by, for example, expanding any reclaimed German New Guinea at the expense of the adjacent Dutch part of that island.

The magnanimity imposed by circumstances on Germany's policy toward the Dutch colonial empire did not extend to Belgium's. All German colonial planning had included the return of former German East Africa, and this implied that Belgium would have to give up Ruanda-Urundi, her share of that colony.[31] Beyond this, however, many Germans cast covetous eyes on the heart of Africa, the Belgian Congo proper. This will become apparent from an examination of the German colonial schemes that flowered in the heyday of German victories.

At the end of May and beginning of June, the position of the German Foreign Ministry was discussed. Ribben-

30. Ribbentrop to Ott, May 20, 1940, *German Documents D*, 9, No. 280.

31. Little in the record gives any indications of German interest in, or even awareness of, the tiny Kionga triangle at the mouth of the Rovuma River that Portugal had acquired from German East Africa. See note 91.

trop met with two of his advisers, Karl Ritter and Carl Clodius (both primarily concerned with economic matters) on May 29, and in the following days the latter defined their views in separate memoranda.[32] Clodius wanted all former German colonies returned with the Belgian Congo added in, the resulting colonial empire to be economically united with the Greater German economic sphere in Europe.[33] This scheme would have assured Germany of large supplies of certain important raw materials; but Ritter obviously felt some doubts on this score, especially as regards Germany's critical need for vegetable fats, as well as on account of the geographical awkwardness of the resulting construction. He therefore urged that French Equatorial Africa and possibly British Nigeria also be included in what would then become a really coherent central African empire. Admiral Kurt Fricke, chief of plans and operations for the German navy, had somewhat similar, if more grandiose, ideas. Eschewing any desire for bases in the Western Hemisphere or in the Asian and Australian area, Fricke also wanted a solid central African empire, but drew its boundaries more generously to include, in addition to the Congo and French Equatorial Africa, all French territories south of the mouth of the Senegal. This would have included Dakar, French Guinea, the Ivory Coast, Dahomey, and large parts of the French Sudan and Niger territories. To expand this central African area southwards, by including all or parts of Angola, Northern Rhodesia, Nyassaland, or Mozambique, he was prepared to give up

32. Memorandum of Clodius, May 30, 1940, ibid., No. 354; Memorandum of Ritter, June 1, 1940, ibid., No. 367.

33. It must always be kept in mind that the Germans in speaking of Cameroons meant not just the French and British mandates carved out of that colony, but also the "New Cameroons" area ceded to Germany in 1911 and reincorporated in the French colonial empire after the war. This territory is important for an understanding of the developments in 1940 because of two aspects otherwise not readily apparent from contemporary maps: it gave Germany a common border with the Belgian Congo at two points and also made Spanish Guinea (Rio Muni) an enclave surrounded on all three land sides by "German" territory.

Southwest Africa in exchange, this latter view perhaps strengthened by Fricke's general aversion to isolated enclaves.[34] With variations, similar demands were urged by the navy throughout 1940.

While his subordinates were performing surgical operations on the African map, Hitler himself had not yet spelled out his demands. In a public interview with Karl von Wiegand on June 15 he reaffirmed his determination to recover the lost colonies,[35] but a new directive issued by Lammers in his behalf on the same day only urged that the preparations for taking over in Germany's "future colonies" be completed in the shortest possible time.[36] Just what these future colonies, which Epp was said to be almost ready to direct from a new state Colonial Ministry, were to be, the Third Reich's most knowledgeable bureaucrat failed to specify, in part because this had not yet been determined. There is evidence of some resulting action by those affected,[37] but more precision in Hitler's plans would have to await the course and outcome of his negotiations with Italy and Spain over their entrance into the war as well as with France over its exit from the conflict.

IV.

Italy's coming into the war as France was already leaving necessarily threw the problem of Italian colonial aspirations and Hitler's views on an armistice with France into conflict. On the way to meet the German leaders for a discussion of armistice terms for France, the Italians worked out their colonial demands. They wanted to occupy Tuni-

34. 1. Skl (Fricke), "Raumerweiterungs- und Stützpunktfragen," June 3, 1940, Nürnberg document 041-C, *Trial of the Major War Criminals* (Nürnberg, 1946-48), 34, 242.

35. *Deutscher Kolonial-Dienst*, 5 (1940), No. 7, p. 96.

36. Lammers an die Obersten Reichsbehörden "RM Nr. 1775/40 A," of June 15, 1940, T-77/642/1838547.

37. See the reference to "colonial troops" in the discussion of the projected peacetime army between the commander in chief and chief of staff of the German army in the Halder Diary under June 19, 1940.

sia, French Somaliland, and bases at Algiers, Oran, and Casablanca.[38] This did not suit Hitler, who had to reconcile his desire to secure an armistice with France by refraining from demands that would drive the French—and especially their fleet—into continued alliance with England with both his own colonial wishes and the bait needed for Spain. In his first conference with Mussolini on June 18, therefore, Hitler passed over the specifics to expatiate in general and at length on the importance of a quick agreement with France.[39] On the following day, however, when Ribbentrop and Count Ciano got down to details, the former agreed to Italy's eventual occupation of Tunisia and British Somaliland and possibly Algeria. On Morocco, Ribbentrop, doubtless instructed by Hitler, had other ideas. That was to go to Spain with Germany, not Italy, holding bases there—a subject to be considered in connection with the German-Spanish negotiations. As for the rest of Germany's own colonial demands, Ribbentrop specified the return of all her old colonies, the Belgian Congo, and undefined French colonies in West Africa.[40] India, the Dutch East Indies, and French Indo-China were specifically ruled out.[41] Since the Italians were already formally at war, without having secured prior German agreement to their demands, they could do little but agree both to the German long-range program as well as to Hitler's desire to secure an armistice with France that left out the colonial question

38. Galeazzo Ciano, *The Ciano Diaries 1939-1943,* ed. Hugh Gibson (Garden City, N.Y.: Doubleday, 1946), June 17, 1940; Italian general staff paper of June 18, 1940 cited in William L. Langer, *Our Vichy Gamble* (New York: Alfred A. Knopf, 1947), p. 48.

39. The German record of this meeting is in *German Documents D,* Vol. 9, No. 479; an Italian record is quoted by Langer, pp. 48 f.; see also Ciano, *Diary,* June 18-19, 1940.

40. Given Ribbentrop's general ignorance of geography, this could have been a reference to Dakar, French Equatorial Africa, or both.

41. Galeazzo Ciano, *Ciano's Diplomatic Papers,* ed. Malcolm Muggeridge (London: Odhams Press, 1948), pp. 373 f. Another Italian record claims that Ribbentrop threw in French Somaliland and a strip to connect Libya with Ethiopia (Langer, p. 49). Other evidence makes this appear plausible.

entirely, thereby postponing it to a future peace settlement. The Spaniards, on the other hand, were as yet outside the conflict and, believing Hitler eager for their entrance, hastened to seek German approval for their share of the spoils of common victory.

Franco presented his bill on June 19. It was exorbitant even by Axis standards. Spain demanded Oran (which the Germans were just promising to Italy), all of Morocco, the extension of Rio de Oro southward by about one hundred miles, and the expansion of Spanish Guinea.[42] The Spanish government might well have been unaware of Germany's aspirations in Morocco or Italy's in Oran, but the demand for an "extension of Spain's coastal territories" in Spanish Guinea showed that Franco's voraciousness greatly exceeded his intelligence. Any increase in the size of Spanish Guinea would necessarily be at the expense of the former German colony of Cameroons that completely surrounds it on the land side; drawing attention to this geographical fact was more likely to lead to German demands for the absorption of Spanish Guinea by their reclaimed colony, than to a generous extension of Spanish territory that would cut off any German colonial empire in central Africa from the Atlantic Ocean. This point was not lost on the Germans—in reply to the requests, the Germans merely took "cognizance of Spain's territorial desires with regard to North Africa," studiously ignoring the Guinea question;[43] and as will be seen, the Germans did in fact soon toy with the idea of acquiring Spanish Guinea to round out their own imperial scheme. In the following weeks, the question of Spanish intervention did not seem acute to Hitler. He was not quite sure of what to do next, and in any case did not want to antagonize France right after the British action against the French fleet on July 3. Furthermore,

42. Weizsäcker to Ribbentrop, June 19, 1940, *German Documents D*, Vol. 9, No. 488.

43. Memorandum of Weizsäcker, June 25, 1940, ibid., Vol. 10 (Washington, D.C.: Government Printing Office, 1957), No. 16.

Hitler was very much aware of the difficulty Germany would face in occupying ahead of the British any colonies that France might be asked to cede to Germany. He mentioned the Cameroons to Ciano as an example of this;[44] and in fact, fear of German colonial ambitions appears to have played some part in the Cameroons and adjacent French Equatorial Africa rallying to De Gaulle in the last week of August.[45] This event only reinforced Hitler's determination to withhold the open expression of all colonial claims until they could be enforced on the spot. To the outside world, as well as to his actual or prospective allies, Hitler therefore presented a cautious front, while behind the scenes German colonial preparations proceeded apace.

Before this activity is examined, it would be well to summarize the geographical dimensions of the empire that Hitler visualized at this time. As can be seen from the foregoing, it was to consist essentially of three parts. Across the center of Africa, there was to be a solid belt of German territory, stretching at least from the Cameroons (if not further westward) to the East African coast. Although the borders of this belt were not defined with any degree of finality, certainly the Congo and probably French Equatorial Africa were to be included. In the second place, the former German colony of Southwest Africa was to be reclaimed. Finally, there was to be a group of German bases in Morocco, supplemented as will be shown by bases on the Canary Islands.

The first two of these have cropped up repeatedly in the history of German colonial ambitions presented here. Germany's return to Southwest Africa long remained a part of the colonial plans, and the central African empire was and remained the core of National Socialist colonial thinking. The interest in bases in Morocco and the Canary Islands,

44. Memorandum of Ciano, July 7, 1940, Ciano, *Diplomatic Papers*, p. 376.

45. Charles de Gaulle, *War Memoirs, The Call to Honor 1940-1942*, trans. Jonathan Griffin (New York: Viking Press, 1955), Vol. 1, pp. 112, 116-18.

however, was new, and, though soon dropped, requires some explanation; because in the short time that this hope was entertained it played a wholly disproportionate role in the conduct of the war. The Germans had had interests, both real and imaginary, in Morocco before World War I. It is unlikely that these were related to the revived concern about the area, because German demands about Morocco in World War II always revolved around bases, not the raw materials motivating interest in the rest of the empire envisioned in Berlin. Coupled with the insistence on bases in the Spanish Canary Islands, this concept clearly originated with the German navy—especially its commander Admiral Raeder—and was related to the proposed conduct of naval warfare against Great Britain[46] and potentially against the United States.[47] The idea of bases in Morocco conflicted with Spanish claims even more than Italian hopes; certainly a demand for long-term German establishment in Spain's own Canary Islands was unlikely to strengthen Franco's zeal for participation in the war. These diplomatic questions, however, were held in abeyance during July and August as the Germans tried to knock Britain out of the war by direct blows. At the same time, colonial work under Hitler's directive of June 15 was moving forward.

Before surveying other details of German colonial preparations resumed in the summer of 1940, it is instructive to examine the number of agencies involved. The last of the prewar circulars on the status of preparatory colonial work, that of June 6, 1939, had been distributed to seventeen military offices.[48] When it was decided on July 4, 1940,

46. See Office of Naval Intelligence, *Fuehrer Confeiences on Matters Dealing with the German Navy 1940* (Washington, D.C., 1947), Vol. 2, passim.

47. The German navy in July, 1940, was planning a program for the large scale construction of battleships *after* the defeat of England—for use against whom? See Nürnberg documents NI-12642, 12643, 12644, 12652, 12653, 12746.

48. See the Verteiler of OKW/Ausl VII, "Bericht 4 über den Stand der kolonialen Vorarbeiten," June 6, 1939, T-77/642/1838556.

that the sending out of such secret periodic information circulars should be resumed, twenty-four offices were informed;[49] one more was added when the first one went out four days later.[50] Six were added on July 27, one on August 10, five on September 6, and one on December 30, 1940. In the following year, seven were added on January 21, two on August 4, one on November 20, and one on December 18, 1941; two having been dropped during the year. By the end of 1941, when publication ceased—presumably due to more pressing business in Russia—eighty-one copies were being passed out to forty-seven military agencies, so that whatever else was done, there was surely a lot of filing.

In several conferences, Hitler gave his highest military advisers the general lines within which they were to make their plans. On July 13, he explained to General Halder, the army chief of staff, the extent of the territory that would have to be garrisoned: the African coast (presumably a reference to bases in Morocco) and the French and Belgian Congo to round out Germany's central African belt.[51] On the same day he laid down the military policy for these colonies to General Keitel, the Chief of the High Command of the Armed Forces (OKW). There would be no military section in the future colonial ministry. The military forces in the colonies would be under the control of the OKW. They would not be modelled on the pre-World War I colonial units. Instead, regular German army units would be stationed in the colonies for short periods of time. Germans living in the colonies could perform only their reserve training with such units; they would carry out their military service obligations inside Germany. The prohibition against recruiting natives was reaffirmed.[52] Hitler's

49. OKW/Ausl VII, "Nr. 12456/40geh.," July 4, 1940, ibid., frame 1838546.

50. OKW/Ausl. VII, "Koloniale Unterrichtung Nr. I," July 8, 1940, T-77/643/1838854. The following statistics are taken from the distribution lists attached to the subsequent issues, all on roll 643.

51. Halder Diary, July 13, 1940; see also ibid., August 23, 1940.

52. The full text of this directive is included in OKW/WFSt/L,

more detailed orders went out a week later. Units of all three services were to be stationed in the colonies according to plans to be worked out exclusively by the military. Small offices within the OKW and the three service headquarters would do the planning in close cooperation, while the possibility of a separate large military office for the colonies was left open for the future. In all this, the section "Foreign States" (Ausland) of OKW was to play the central role. Other OKW offices, advised by the Colonial Ministry, would help on the development of general directives. Within the framework prescribed by these, the three services would work out their orders.[53] To keep the anticipated jurisdictional struggles within limits, Keitel laid down the ground rules allocating spheres of activity inside the OKW and among the three services on July 31.[54]

In accordance with these directives, special sections for colonial preparations were established in the OKW, the army, the air force, and the navy.[55] In the OKW, a variety of general problems regarding colonial policy was under consideration.[56] Some of these, as well as the more immediate questions of a colonial law and the occupation of prospective colonies, were discussed with Epp and will be reviewed in connection with an examination of the latter's activities. A major concern continued to be the selection and preparation of adequate numbers of doctors and vet-

---

"Kolonial-Ordnung der Wehrmacht, Erster Vorarbeitsentwurf vom 1. 1. 1941," T-77/642/1838272-273; a summary was distributed in OKW/Ausl VII, "Koloniale Unterrichtung Nr. III," July 31, 1940, T-77/643/1838846.

53. OKW/Ausl VII, "Koloniale Unterrichtung Nr. II," July 27, 1940, T-77/643/1838848-849.

54. OKW/Ausl VII, "Koloniale Unterrichtung Nr. III," July 31, 1940, ibid., frames 1838845-846. (Some of the subsequent issues of this series amended the original list.)

55. See, OKW/Wi Rü Amt, "Vorläufiger Arbeitsplan der Sondergruppe 'Koloniale Vorarbeiten' der Abt. W/WiRüAmt," July 9, 1940, T-77/642/1838207-211; Halder Diary, July 5, 1940; OKW/Ausl VII, "Nr. 13076/40geh.," Aug. 1, 1940, T-77/642/1838531; OKW/Ausl VII, "Koloniale Unterrichtung Nr. VI," Oct. 5, 1940, T-77/643/183837.

56. See the seven-page memorandum "Zur Kolonialfrage" of June 27, 1940, distributed by OKW/Ausl VII under "Nr. 12531/40geh." on July 10, 1940, T-77/642/1838538-545.

erinarians in the field of tropical medicine.[57] Arrangements were also made for the training of officers of the three services in colonial administration, with the first course running from September 3-12, 1940, and others following at least until the eighth in January, 1942.[58] These courses, as well as certain other training activities, were conducted at Hamburg University's Colonial Institute, an old center of colonial studies in Germany that had been reopened in 1939[59] and was expanded by the addition of a special Institute for Colonial Economics in the spring of 1941.[60] In spite of this appearance of feverish activity, Geldern, in an internal conference in the OKW on August 1, 1940, pointed out that in fact the preparations so far had been of a purely theoretical character, that many of the policy questions—such as the kinds of troops to be used—were still open (in spite of Hitler's decrees on the subject), and that the problem to settle next was that of pay and allowances for the colonial garrison. This issue was gravely and lengthily discussed, but even with the distribution of tables of the pre-World War I pay scales of three of the German colonies no decisions were made.[61]

The German Army General Staff, however, realizing that it might be called upon at any moment to provide garrisons for a far-flung colonial empire, was giving serious

57. This question is touched on repeatedly in the "Koloniale Unterrichtungen," beginning with No. II of July 27, 1940, T-77/643/183849-850.

58. OKW/Ausl VII, "Koloniale Unterrichtung Nr. IV," Aug. 10, 1940, ibid., frame 1838843 and "Koloniale Unterrichtung Nr. 17," December 18, 1941, ibid., frame 183877.

59. See the "Verzeichnis der kolonialwissenschaftlichen Schriften und Aufsätze von Mitgliedern und Mitarbeitern im Kolonial-Institut der Hansischen Universität zu Hamburg," zusammengestellt aus Anlass der Wiedereröffnung des Kolonial-Instituts (Hamburg: Hans Christians, 1939).

60. Dr. Heinz-Dietrich Ortlieb, "Lebenslauf," Oct. 5, 1941, T-77/642/1838476.

61. Major Dr. von Reumont, "Bericht über die Besprechung bei W Allg am 1. August 1940, Betr. Besoldung innerhalb der Wehrmacht für die Kolonien," T-77/642/1838524-530. See also OKW/Wehrmachtshaushalts-Abteilung, "Ausgaben für die kolonialen Vorarbeiten," Aug. 14, 1940, ibid., frame 1838523.

thought to the creation of an expeditionary force in the leisurely interval between the French campaign and the preparations for the attack on Russia when the desultory cross-Channel invasion plans could not keep it busy. Originally the army planned for only two battalions of four companies each, but this was soon increased to ten battalions, half of them motorized, for a total of ten thousand men.[62] The troops for these units were to come from the divisions scheduled for deactivation in the summer of 1940 and from the Replacement Army. Although the subject was repeatedly discussed in high army circles,[63] the reorientation of German military manpower planning in August and September, 1940, caused by the decision to attack Russia made the implementation of such plans practically impossible.[64] After the beginning of September, as the army was to be built up to 180, later 200, divisions for the coming invasion of Russia, evidence on the preparation of a colonial expeditionary force almost disappears. The army merely tried to keep informed on the course of political and diplomatic discussions in case a sudden demand for colonial contingents should arise. What actual preparations the army did undertake, in preparing a tropical uniform for example,[65] came to benefit only the Italian colonial empire via Rommel's Africa-Corps.

In the meantime, the political and administrative preparations for Germany's empire seemed to be moving into high gear at Epp's Colonial Policy Office. At the beginning of July a law establishing the Reich Ministry of Colonies

62. Halder Diary, July 5 and 19, 1940. It is worth noting that these units were originally to await their colonial assignments in Bergen (Norway), where tropical outfits, if issued, would have been singularly inappropriate.

63. See Halder Diary, July 22 and 25, August 12, 1940.

64. The author has discussed the immediate repercussions on manpower planning of the decision to attack Russia in his *Germany and the Soviet Union, 1939-1941* (Leyden: Brill, 1954), pp. 118 f. and in his "Der Deutsche Entschluss zum Angriff auf die Sowjetunion," *Vierteljahrshefte für Zeitgeschichte*, 1 (1953), 302, 314.

65. OKW, Ausl VII, "Koloniale Unterrichtung Nr. VI." Oct. 5, 1940, T-77/643/1838838.

had apparently been drafted; the text has not turned up, but its publication was declared imminent.[66] Epp himself was to become Colonial Minister. A colonial law (Reichskolonialgesetz) was also in preparation. It was to be ready by August 1—an estimate that proved to be many months off—but was to be published only after peace had been signed. Epp, who expected peace to break out at any moment, believed that German occupation of the colonies would proceed peacefully over a period of about six months, with German units and administrators replacing those of the enemy powers by stages starting with the coastal areas. The only substantive colonial policy Epp had decided upon by this time was that in the early period of German administration large tourist and hunting parties were not to be allowed. Such rosy prospects suffered early set-backs. By July 27 it was clear that the draft colonial law could not be ready in time, because there were still arguments about article six concerning the military command structure in the colonies.[67] At the same time, it was decided that publication of the law on the Colonial Ministry and of Epp's appointment should be postponed, although the Ministry was being formed in the Colonial Policy Office.[68] While the dispute about article six apparently involved the relationship of troops in the colonies to the colonial governors, deferring the announcement of Epp's appointment may well have been caused by Hitler's general uncertainty in July and especially by his reluctance to offend France. This speculation is substantiated by Geldern's statement at the conference of August 1 that "the establishment of the Colonial Ministry has been temporarily postponed for foreign policy reasons."[69] This, of

66. This and the following in OKW/Ausl VII, "Koloniale Unterrichtung Nr. I," July 8, 1940, ibid., frames 1838852-853.

67. Since only the ninth draft of this law, circulated at the end of 1940, is available, the draft under discussion in the summer cannot be reviewed.

68. OKW/Ausl VII, "Koloniale Unterrichtung Nr. II," July 27, 1940, ibid., frame 1838849.

69. Major Dr. von Reumont, "Bericht über die Besprechung bei W

course, did not prevent the continuation of internal discussions. On the contrary, knowing that the proposed colonial law had by August 9 already received its *tenth* and by no means final reading,[70] we can be certain that the Party and military bureaucrats were hard at work. The needed guidebooks were in preparation: in the middle of August the Colonial Policy Office announced the forthcoming appearance of a new series of publications on colonial policy. The first was to be entitled "Colonial Policy from A to Z" and the second "A New Colonial Policy." By 1942, when these appeared, titles and purposes had changed,[71] but that was far in the future. At the moment, Epp's subordinates were busy with other urgent projects. Not only was further work necessary on the colonial law, but drafts had to be prepared of laws concerning foreigners resident in German colonies, colonial administrative procedure, colonial officials' pay, colonial budgets, judicial procedures involving Germans, judicial procedures involving natives, mining, police, and so forth.[72] All the activity led to rumors of profitable employment opportunities, and floods of applications for military and civilian positions in the colonial sphere poured in.[73]

The refusal of Great Britain to agree with Hitler's estimate that Germany had already won the war and the signs

---

Allg. am 1. August . . . ," T-77/642/1838525. The same reason was again given on September 6, see "Koloniale Unterrichtung Nr. V" cited in note 72, below.

70. OKW/Ausl VII, "Koloniale Unterrichtung Nr. IV," Aug. 10, 1940, T-77/643/1838843.

71. *Deutscher Kolonial-Dienst,* Vol. 5, inside cover of the Aug. 15, 1940 issue. German title of the series: Koloniale Politik, Schriften des Kolonialpolitischen Amtes, of the proposed books: Koloniale Politik von A bis Z, and: Neue Kolonialpolitik. For the titles as actually issued, see n. 127.

72. OKW/Ausl VII, "Koloniale Unterrichtung Nr. V," Sept. 6, 1940, T-77/643/1838840-841. Other agencies, such as the Ministry of Finance, helped draft these laws, see OKW/Ausl VII, "Koloniale Unterrichtung Nr. VII," Oct. 25, 1940, ibid., frame 1838834.

73. OKW/Ausl VII, "Koloniale Unterrichtung Nr. VI," Oct. 5, 1940, T-77/643/1838837. A large number of vitae of aspiring colonial officers and officials sent to the OKW/Wi Rü Amt, 1940-1943, may be found in T-77/642/1838398-1838496.

increased American willingness and ability to aid England not only meant that the eager colonialists had to content themselves with places on the waiting lists, but also reemphasized to Hitler the need for military action against England. Of the proposed operations, one of the most important and most promising was the seizure of Gibraltar and the crossing of the Straits to North Africa. This scheme necessarily increased Hitler's interest in Spain's entrance into the war; and that, in turn, required a reexamination of German, Spanish, and Italian colonial ambitions. Spain's importance to the Germans had temporarily increased, though France—now more hostile to England than ever—might become an alternative or complementary ally in the conflict.

V.

The Spanish government had submitted its demands in June; these were now subjected to renewed scrutiny leading to the negotiations of September and October 1940. The German Ambassador to Spain, Eberhard von Stohrer, had reviewed the pros and cons of Spanish intervention when in Berlin at the beginning of August, but, like the official German reply to the Spanish government, had not commented on the details of the Spanish demands.[74] Franco became fearful that Berlin's silence might mean that Spain would not be invited to share the colonial booty and recalled "the aspirations and claims of Spain" in "the disposition of the North African territories" to the Germans indirectly through Mussolini[75] and directly through other approaches.[76] The Germans, on August 26, extended an in-

74. Memorandum by Stohrer, Aug. 8, 1940, *German Documents D*, Vol. 10, No. 313. This is No. 1 in the State Department's collection *The Spanish Government and the Axis* (Washington, D.C.: Government Printing Office, 1946).

75. Franco to Mussolini, Aug. 15, 1940, *German Documents D*, Vol. 10, No. 346; *The Spanish Government and the Axis*, No. 2.

76. Herbert Feis, *The Spanish Story* (New York: Alfred A. Knopf, 1948), pp. 72 f.

vitation to Serrano Suñer, Franco's brother-in-law, to Berlin for a discussion of Spanish intervention and aspirations. On the following day, Ambassador Stohrer sent his proposal for a German-Spanish agreement to Berlin. In regard to colonial matters—on which he had clearly received some new information in or from Berlin—Stohrer proposed that Spain would receive Tangier, Oran, and French Morocco with some exceptions. In Morocco Germany was to secure both certain (as yet unspecified) ports, and there as well as in the rest of Spanish Africa Germany expected a share both of former French and British mining property and of any Spanish mines. The ambassador further proposed that the Spanish claims to expansion of Rio de Oro and Guinea could be tied together: Germany would agree to the former in exchange for adding either Spanish Guinea itself or the island of Fernando Po to Cameroons.[77] This scheme did not include the Canary Islands demand of Hitler that was as yet unknown to Stohrer, but even the Morocco terms were certain to cause a shock to the Spaniards whom Hitler had assured that "Germany had no interests of any kind in Morocco except the economic ones" as recently as June 16.[78] It does seem that prior to Suñer's visit the Germans had decided to agree to the requested southward extension of Rio de Oro.[79] Hitler explained the line he planned to take to General Halder on September 14, namely "to promise Spaniards everything they want, regardless of whether the promise can be kept."[80]

77. Stohrer to Ribbentrop, Aug. 27, 1940, *German Documents* D, Vol. 10, No. 405.

78. Memorandum of Conversation between Hitler and General Vigón, June 16, 1940, ibid., Vol. 9, No. 456.

79. This is the only way to make sense out of a confusing entry in the Halder Diary for Sept. 16, 1940. The explanatory note in the English edition is meaningless.

80. Halder Diary, Sept. 14, 1940. The published notes on colonial plans by Hasso von Etzdorf, Foreign Ministry representative to the High Command of the German Army, appear to belong in this context. They list intended divisions of the Ministry for Colonies and some alternative schemes for the partition of Africa, *German Documents D,* Vol. 11, No. 16.

The records of Suñer's conversations in Berlin[81] show that in fact Hitler did not follow quite so cynical a policy. Though willing to agree in principle to certain of the Spanish demands, Hitler and Ribbentrop insisted on the cession of one of the Canary Islands—which Suñer flatly refused even to consider—and on two bases and extensive economic rights in Morocco. Since these demands were combined with other requests for economic concessions in Spain itself as well as its North African empire, even such pro-Axis Spaniards as Franco and Suñer might slowly have begun to comprehend that Spain's place in the New Order of Greater Germany would be that of an insignificant and exploited satellite. Directly relevant for an understanding of German colonial aspirations is the fact that by this time the concept of the large central African empire, with naval bases in the Canaries and on the Morocco coast to assure access to it, had become sufficiently firm in the mind of Hitler and his entourage that they were unwilling to let immediate objectives in the war against Britain interfere with it. For the phantom of empire in Africa, they would sacrifice Spanish cooperation in the assault on Gibraltar.[82] This choice was, however, not fully understood by the Germans at the time; for when Ribbentrop went to Rome right after Suñer's visit, he expressed, possibly truthfully, the belief that Spain would soon enter the war under the conditions Germany had prescribed.[83] The diplomatic documents of subsequent weeks, nevertheless, point up the real rift: Franco's letter to Hitler of September 22 argues vehemently against German bases in Morocco;[84] Hitler was quite dubious about Spain when talking to Ciano on Sep-

81. See the excellent summary in Feis, pp. 78-85, and *German Documents D,* Vol. 11, Nos. 30, 63, 66, 67, 70.

82. See Franco's later complaints to Mussolini on 12 February 1941, Ciano, *Diplomatic Papers,* pp. 424 f., 428 f.

83. Memorandum of Schmidt, Sept. 20, 1940, Nürnberg document 1842-PS, *Trial of the Major War Criminals,* 28, 577 ff.; *German Documents D,* Vol. 11, Nos. 73, 79.

84. *The Spanish Government and the Axis,* No. 5; *German Documents D,* Vol. XI, No. 88. See also the spirited argument between Ribbentrop and Suñer on Sept. 24, 1940, ibid., No. 97.

tember 28 and did not even mention Franco's aspirations on the Guinea coast in listing the Spanish demands.[85] The Germans would make one more effort to reconcile their ambitions with those of Spain, but the alternative possibility of an alliance with Vichy France would only reinforce Hitler's determination to make no firm commitments on the future of the French colonial empire. Any promises would probably leak out and merely push French Africa into the arms of Great Britain or De Gaulle.[86]

While the German-Spanish negotiations of September, 1940, led to no agreement, in part because of conflicting colonial ambitions, those simultaneously conducted between Germany and Japan for the Tripartite Pact also came close to foundering over colonial questions. The Japanese, returning to their position in the pre-war negotiations with Germany, insisted on the cession of Germany's former Pacific colonial empire to themselves. Not only the islands north of the equator under Japanese mandate, but also German New Guinea, the Bismarck Archipelago, the Solomons, Nauru, and German Samoa were to go to Japan after the defeat of Great Britain and the Dominions.[87] Only after the German negotiators in Tokyo agreed to this and other concessions—without the authorization of the German Foreign Minister—was Japan prepared to sign. To what extent the colonial question had been a real stumbling-block in 1940 is not quite clear from the evidence; by the spring of 1941, however, officials in the German Foreign Ministry who had not been informed of the concessions already secretly made to Tokyo suggested that these territories might well be promised to Japan to induce her to enter the war against England.[88]

It was this idea, the recruitment of allies in the war

85. *German Documents D,* Vol. 11, No. 124.

86. *The Spanish Government and the Axis,* Nos. 12 and 13.

87. Johanna M. Menzel, "Der geheime deutsch-japanische Notenaustausch zum Dreimächtepakt," *Vierteljahrshefte für Zeitgeschichte,* V (1957), 182-93, especially pp. 185 f. and 193.

88. Ibid., p. 187, n. 20. I am indebted to Professor Menzel for additional details on this point. Some documents on this episode have been published in *German Documents D,* Vol. 11, Nos. 74, 82, 121.

against England, that lay behind Hitler's meetings with Franco and Pétain in October, 1940. Only the colonial aspect of these conversations will be considered here. The evidence shows that although Hitler was willing to make concessions to both, there were certain minimal colonial wishes he expected to realize under any circumstances. He would secure a central African colonial empire for which either France or England (by exchanges) would foot the bill. Germany would insist on bases in North West Africa—though Hitler might have been willing to settle for *either* one of the Canary Islands or a port in Morocco instead of both.[89] As for the fate of the French empire in Africa, that would depend in part on the willingness of France to cooperate in the war against England; but in any case, nothing beyond the retrocession of Germany's former colonial empire would be announced now for fear of repercussions in France itself as well as in North Africa. Examining the schemes presented by the Germans alternately to Spain, France, and Italy for the switching and exchanging of territories in Africa, one cannot avoid the impression that at this time the dream of African empire was firmly impressed on Hitler's mind.[90] The boundaries waxed and waned with the diplomatic tides in the late fall and winter of 1940; the intention remained throughout. Even after the failure of the whole German diplomatic effort, the central African scheme remained the core of German aspirations to be communicated to the Soviet Union on Molotov's visit to Berlin in November.[91] These talks were designed only to

89. *Halder Diary,* Oct. 15, 1940. In either case, possession, not lease, would be required.

90. *Halder Diary,* Oct. 8 and 15, 1940, Nov. 1, 1940, Dec. 9 and 15, 1940; Conversation between Hitler and Franco, Oct. 23, 1940, *The Spanish Government and the Axis,* pp. 24 f; Langer, p. 95; Otto Abetz, *Das Offene Problem* (Cologne: Greven Verlag, 1951), p. 158; Conversation between Hitler and Mussolini, Oct. 28, 1940, Ciano, *Diplomatic Papers,* pp. 401, 403; Feis, pp. 96 f. *German Documents D,* Vol. 11, Nos. 98, 102, 104, 108, 112, 116, 117, 149, 150, 175, 199, 207, 208, 212, 220, 221, 224, 227, 235, 246, 294, 352, and pp. 466-67.

91. Ciano-Ribbentrop conversation, Nov. 4, 1940, Ciano, *Diplomatic Papers,* p. 406; German draft protocol for the pact with Russia, Nov. 9,

clear the air until Germany could mount her attack in the East; African problems were touched on very lightly. Of more immediate concern to the Germans in Africa was the apparently imminent demise of Italy's colonial venture in North Africa through the British offensive into Libya at the beginning of December, 1940; and many of the preparations for German colonial activity were funnelled into the long, costly, and eventually futile endeavour to salvage Mussolini's empire by employment of the Africa-Corps.[92]

VI.

The failure of Hitler's diplomatic activities in the late fall of 1940 in no way dampened the enthusiasm of the colonial planners; on the contrary, once the Third Reich's bureaucrats had been let loose on the subject and individuals assigned the usually overlapping jurisdictions, the whole machinery ground on undisturbed by reality. In this work, many facets of German colonial thought were exposed to view. The German empire was to be blessed with its own National Socialist Party organization, prepared by the Foreign Section (AO) of the Party.[93] A conference at the OKW on November 20 allocated the preparation of

---

1940, *Das Nationalsozialistische Deutschland und die Sowjetunion 1939-1941,* German ed. E. M. Carroll and F. T. Epstein (Berlin: Tempelhof, 1948), p. 197; see also ibid., pp. 251, 259, 282.

A memorandum by Dr. Bielfeld, chief of the section of the German Foreign Ministry dealing with Africa, of Nov. 6, 1940 sketches the outlines of an ambitious central African empire including substantial parts of British and French West Africa, as well as French Equatorial Africa, the Belgian Congo, Uganda, Kenya, Zanzibar, and Northern Rhodesia. Alone among German colonial planners Dr. Bielfeld thought of the Kionga triangle; he expected to arrive at an understanding with Portugal. *German Documents D,* Vol. 11, No. 298.

92. For early preparatory steps, see OKW/WiRüAmt, "Wehrwirtschaftliche Organisation in Nordafrika," Oct. 29, 1940, T-77/642/1838192; OKW/WiRüAmt, "Wehrwirtschaftsorganisation für besonderen Zweck," Nov. 1, 1940, ibid., frames 1838203-206.

93. Bekanntgabe B 75/40 in the Reichsverfügungsblatt des Stellvertreters des Führers 33/40 of Nov. 12, 1940. This item and a number of others on colonial subjects are reprinted in the *Vorschriftenhandbuch der Hitlerjugend* issued by the Reichsjugendführung (Berlin: Mittler, 1942), 3, 2360-64.

colonial uniforms and equipment to the army and of colonial barracks to the navy.[94] By November, 1940, the Germans had come to realize that other powers had had prior experiences in the African colonial field and that the relevant files of the French, Belgian, and Dutch colonial ministries had fallen under their control earlier that year. A general scramble ensued in which various agencies—primarily the Party's Colonial Policy Office and the military—sought control of these files. Although the documentation on the scramble is very extensive, there is no indication that much was learned from the files eventually concentrated in several special collecting centers.[95] It may be, however, that information gleaned from such sources was utilized in the various training courses already mentioned or in the series of advanced courses instituted by OKW and also held in Hamburg, beginning in March, 1941.[96] More concrete lessons from the experience of others could be gathered by those trainees of the police and SS who went to Rome in person to study the Italian colonial administration.[97] Some of the special units for the colonies were ready to go—on December 18, 1940, Epp inspected a trained detachment of 350 forest rangers (Forstschutzkommando).[98]

94. OKW/AWA, "849/40g Betr.: Verwaltungsangelegenheiten der Gesamtwehrmacht in den Kolonien," Jan. 8, 1941, T-77/642/1838521.

95. OKW/Ausl VII, "Koloniale Unterrichtung Nr. VIII," Nov. 25, 1940, T-77/643/1838828; "Koloniale Unterrichtung Nr. IX," Dec. 30, 1940, T-77/643/183825; RMdL u. ObdL, "Nr. 7520/4.41, Betr. Koloniale Vorbereitung," April 25, 1941, T-77/642/1838506; OKW/Ausl VII, "Nr. 1954/41geh," May 16, 1941, T-77/642/1838507 and the attached note of May 19, frames 1838508-509; OKW/WiRüAmt to Ritter von Epp, June 7, 1941, T-77/642/1838179; Kolonialpolitisches Amt to OKW/WiRüAmt June 13, 1941, T-77/642/1838090-91; OKW/Ausl VII, "Koloniale Unterrichtung Nr. 13," Aug. 4, 1941, T-77/643/1838798-799; OKW/Ausl VII, "Koloniale Unterrichtung Nr. 14," Aug. 27, 1941, T-77/643/1838792-793; OKW/Ausl VII, "Koloniale Unterrichtung Nr. 15," Sept. 23, 1941, T-77/643/1838785-786.

96. OKW/Ausl VII, "Koloniale Unterrichtung Nr. 11," Feb. 12, 1941, T-77/643/1838814.

97. OKW/Ausl VII, "Koloniale Unterrichtung Nr. VIII," Nov. 25, 1940, ibid., frame 1838832.

98. OKW/Ausl VII, "Koloniale Unterrichtung Nr. IX," Dec. 30, 1940, ibid., frame 1838826. The subject of forestry in the colonies—especially in

A year later, he inspected the second police commando of 300 and checked on their proficiency at bellowing orders in Suaheli and Haussa; the first commando was by then already serving in Libya.[99]

Of more general interest for an understanding of German colonial ideas than the various specific preparations is the series of discussions on colonial policy in the winter 1940-41. These revolved about three problems: the proposed colonial law, the colonial regulations of the armed forces, and the question of using native troops in the colonies. These three issues were closely related and will be examined together. They were to be discussed at a conference on January 9, 1941, that was to be attended by representatives of various sections of the OKW and the three services and preceded by study of the key issues.[100] One of those brought up first was that of Askaris, of native troops. In spite of Hitler's insistence that there were not to be any, the military were still examining the possibility.[101] In the first draft of the "Colonial Regulations of the Armed Forces" (Kolonial-Ordnung der Wehrmacht) Hitler's previously cited order of July 13, 1940, prohibiting Askaris is quoted in full, but it is immediately followed by the state-

---

Cameroons—was of great interest to the Germans, in part because of the propagandizing activities of Franz Heske, professor at Hamburg University and director of the Reichsinstitut für ausländische und koloniale Forstwirtschaft. Heske published many studies in the field and constantly sent memoranda on the subject to state and Party agencies (e. g. his "Denkschrift über die kriegsentscheidende Bedeutung der kolonialen Vorarbeiten" of Apr. 22, 1941 in T-77/642/1838107-111).

99. OKW/Ausl VII, "Koloniale Unterrichtung Nr. 17," Dec. 18, 1941, T-77/643/1838774. See also William L. Shirer, *Berlin Diary* (New York: Alfred A. Knopf, 1942), entry for July 17, 1940, p. 360. Details on the Office for Colonial Police (Kolonialpolizeiamt der Ordnungspolizei) may be found in Hans Joachim Neufeldt, "Entstehung und Organisation des Hauptamtes Ordnungspolizei," in *Zur Geschichte der Ordnungspolizei 1936-1945* (= Schriften des Bundesarchivs 3) (Boppard: Boldt, 1957), pp. 73 f.

100. OKW/WFSt/L, "4228/40, Betr. Kol. Vorarbeiten," Dec. 18, 1940, T-77/642/1838397. The meeting was to be held in General Warlimont's office, but he did not attend.

101. OKW/Ausl VII, "Koloniale Unterrichtung Nr. IX," Dec. 30, 1940, T-77/643/1838825.

ment that Epp considered Askaris necessary in the tropical areas. Not only that, but for probably the only time in his long and ignoble career, Keitel, the Chief of the OKW, signified that he, too, differed with Hitler. The draft asserts that the question is still open and that planning is to proceed on the basis of both alternative possibilities.[102] The subject was one of the major topics canvassed at the January 9 conference; all apparently agreed on the need for Askaris.[103]

A detailed memorandum on the subject of native troops, by an officer with colonial experience attached to Epp's office, provided the basis for the discussion,[104] and copies of it were distributed after the session. Its contents deserve summarizing.[105] Aside from the financial savings involved, native troops were declared necessary for Germany as for all other European power with colonies in the tropics, first, because of their military superiority due to the natives' greater acclimatization and familiarity with the peculiarities of the terrain. Tropical diseases furnish the second reason. The European troops are much more susceptible to these, and the percentage of men dropping out during a campaign would be inordinately high in any white unit. The preventive equipment, in the form of elaborate tents, nets, etc., moreover, would practically immobilizc a European unit. Finally, the racial question—undoubtedly the basis of Hitler's opposition to the use of native troops—was turned around to support the opposite contention. If regular German army units were stationed in the colonies, even the strictest regulations would not keep the soldiers from sexual relations with native women. This would, in itself,

102. OKW/WFSt/L, "Kolonial-Ordnung der Wehrmacht, Erster Vorarbeitsentwurf vom 1. 1. 1941," T-77/642/1838273.

103. OKW/WiRüAmt (Rentsch), "Aktennotiz zur Besprechung bei L am 9. Januar 1941," Jan. 10, 1941, ibid., frames 1838230-231.

104. OKW/Ausl VII, "Koloniale Unterrichtung Nr. X," Jan. 21, 1941, T-77/643/1838819.

105. Major (ret.) Eymael, "Weisse und farbige Truppen in tropischen Kolonien," no date, T-77/642/1838511-520; covering note of Jan. 16, 1941 on frame 1838510.

be a serious offense that would lead to many soldiers being sent back to serve sentences in German penal institutions; in addition, there would be children of mixed ancestry, always the special butt of German racist thinking. A variety of reasons precluded the establishment of public houses; the only solution was to send only German officers and noncommissioned officers, preferably married, and with their dependents allowed to live in the colonies. This complex of racial and sexual questions was examined on January 9. Epp's office apparently submitted a draft "Blood-Protection Law" (Blutschutzgesetz) modelled on the Nürnberg laws with their jail penalties for race defilement (Rassenschande), because objections were raised against the proposed heavy penalties in view of the extraordinary conditions in the colonies. The proposal to send only married men also created difficulties—clearly these problems required further thought and inter-departmental negotiations.

However exciting the arguments over the special racial problems provoked by the stationing of German troops in the colonies, there were other issues deserving of attention. These were summarized in the "Colonial Regulations of the Armed Forces" and the proposed Colonial Law.[106] The proposed Colonial Law, now in its ninth draft, contained eleven articles. The first two declare the colonies German territory and a part of Germany's economic system. The third classifies the population into Germans, natives, and resident foreigners. The fourth establishes the competence of the Minister of Colonies for all aspects of colonial administration. Article five provides for governors appointed by the Fuehrer for each colony and acting in accordance

106. The material used in the following discussion is contained in the modified edition of the previously cited first draft of the Kolonial-Ordnung. Changed only slightly from the prior version, this text formed the basis of discussion on January 9 and may be found in T-77/642/1838235-265. The Colonial Law is included in this as an appendix. The report on the discussion, with a list of those in attendance, is on frames 1838230-233.

with the directives of the Minister of Colonies. The sixth article dealt with the role of the military; Epp's proposal is not included in the available copy, the OKW's views will be given below. Articles seven, eight, nine, and eleven cover legal questions; article ten provides for the Reichsmark as the basis for the colonial currency.

This colonial law had been under discussion for about half a year; the Colonial Regulations of the Armed Forces, on the other hand, were out as a first draft as the basis for further thought. Nevertheless, this document contains sections of real interest that should be mentioned in spite of their tentative nature. Colonial empire is defined purely in terms of African territory acquired primarily as a source of raw materials. The highest military authorities in the colonies were to be appointed by the OKW. The OKW proposed that their position be defined in the Colonial Law as subordinate to higher military headquarters, that is, the OKW. The military functions of the governors would be restricted to control of the police and support of the military in time of war. The titles, jurisdictions, and duties of the military commanders in the colonies were defined in terms that combined the status of the military district commanders in Germany (Wehrkreisbefehlshaber) with direction of operations in wartime. In other words, there was to be a unified command under OKW direction. Clearly the OKW wished from the start to assure itself of a position in each colony analogous to the one it was striving to attain in Germany itself. Many of the details of military regulations and procedures had not yet been prepared, for only the agency having jurisdiction is indicated in the draft. The various offices were to submit their detailed contributions by the middle of March 1941.[107]

In the period between the January conference and the

107. The only contribution of that period in the available files is: OKW/WiRüAmt/Wi II, "Beitrag zur Kolonialordnung, Vorentwurf zur Verteilung der Aufgaben auf die Abteilungen des Wi Rü Amtes," March 30, 1941 (1942 in the original, doubtless a typing error), T-77/642/1838266-268.

attack on Russia in June 1941 there were several cross-currents in the field of colonial planning. For reasons not revealed by the documents, Epp decided that the sessions on the Colonial Law, held periodically since the previous summer, would be suspended until further notice—which never came.[108] This step, however, did not imply a suspension of operations in the Colonial Policy Office; on the contrary, the evidence indicates that all sorts of organizational and substantive activity continued to occupy Epp and his associates.[109] Various preparations were also carried forward in the sections of the OKW[110] but clearly with less urgency than before, as the forthcoming Balkan and Russian operations demanded attention. Furthermore, Colonel Geldern, the moving colonial spirit in the OKW, spent the spring gathering impressions in the fighting in Libya and did not return to disseminate his findings until the second half of July.

Only the German navy—still opposed to the Russian adventure and still eager for naval bases in Africa for the war against England—urged on Hitler an active policy in the colonial sphere by cooperation with France.[111] For a short time, in May of 1941, these hopes seemed attainable. The uprising against British influence in Iraq, following on the British defeat in the Balkans, made the Germans eager for the use of bases in Syria; and the subsequent fight of the Vichy French army in Syria against British and Free French forces showed Hitler that here was a potential ally of more steadfast determination than he had imagined. Negotiations between Germany and Vichy, culminating in a conversation between Hitler and Admiral Darlan, can-

108. OKW/Ausl VII, "Koloniale Unterrichtung Nr. X," Jan. 21, 1941, T-77/643/1838818.

109. See, e.g., the organizational changes and the dispute over the uniform of colonial officials in OKW/Ausl VII, "Koloniale Unterrichtung Nr. 11," Feb. 12, 1941, ibid., frame 1838815.

110. See the Koloniale Unterrichtungen 10 and 11 cited above.

111. Conference of March 18, 1941, in: *Fuehrer Conference on Matters Dealing with the German Navy*, 1941, I, 36.

vassed the possibilities of joint operations against Britain. Darlan was quite interested in an arrangement whereby entrance into the war on Germany's side would assure France, among other things, of either retention of her own colonial empire or compensation at the expense of a defeated Britain, but nothing came of these grandiose designs. Darlan was repudiated at Vichy, and Hitler could not overcome his distrust and distaste for the French.[112] A renewed approach by the French in July 1941 proposing that the armistice of 1940 be replaced by a peace treaty including a provision for return of the German colonies held by France and leaving open the possibility of other colonial exchanges was rudely rejected by Hitler.[113] When he turned down this French suggestion, Hitler's eyes were firmly rivetted on the Eastern front.

VII.

On June 21, 1941, the day before the attack on Russia, the Chief of the General Staff of the German Army referred in his diary to a discussion about disbanding the army's colonial staff.[114] The army clearly had more pressing responsibilities. In Hitler's mind, the long sought living space in the East was about to be conquered, but there was a residue of the African colonialist dream. At the end of June he emphasized the continental character of Germany's future empire, but stated that this did not imply a renunciation of colonies in the traditional sense: Togo, Cameroons, the Belgian Congo, and perhaps East Africa were to be included.[115] It is worthy of note that the two appendages to the old concept had been dropped—South-

112. On the colonial aspects of this episode, see Langer, pp. 150, 402-12; Ribbentrop-Mussolini—Ciano conversation, May 13, 1941, Nürnberg document 1866—PS, *Trial of the Major War Criminals,* 39, 35; Abetz, pp. 157-59. A good account is in Eberhard Jäckel, *Frankreich in Hitlers Europa* (Stuttgart: Deutsche Verlags-Anstalt, 1966), chap. 10.

113. *Halder Diary,* July 15 and 16, 1941; Abetz, pp. 197 f.

114. *Halder Diary,* June 21, 1941.

115. *Ibid.,* June 30, 1941.

west Africa and the Canary Islands or Morocco bases. The slight success Admiral Raeder had had in drawing Hitler's attention to oceanic questions had been effaced by the fascination of unlimited land conquests. By comparison with the lands in the East, colonies were both less valuable and more precarious possessions, Hitler explained in August.[116] Occasionally he became positively modest; assuming victory in the East, he would be satisfied with return of the Cameroons.[117] His recorded statements in 1942 waver between concern for the difficulty of communication with African colonies as contrasted with space in the East[118] and extravagant hints about ambitions in Africa and beyond.[119]

When Epp submitted a memorandum on the colonial question at the beginning of September 1942 while the German armies were still advancing in South Russia, Hitler commented to his entourage that no colonies elsewhere could compare with those already acquired in the East.[120] The text of this memorandum has not yet turned up, but there is no doubt that some colonial preparations had continued in the intervening months. The evaluation work on the captured French, Belgian, and Dutch colonial archives has already been mentioned. Epp's new Reichskolonial-Institut in Berlin-Grunewald was turning out the future members of the colonial civil service.[121] Plans were made and conferences held to assure common standardized equipment for the civilian and military sectors of the colonial administration.[122] This question was related to the

116. Entry for Aug. 11, 1941, Hugh R. Trevor-Roper (ed.), *Hitler's Table Talk* (London: Weidenfeld, 1953), p. 24.

117. Entry for Oct. 18, 1941, ibid., p. 74. See also Abetz, pp. 219 f.

118. Entry for Feb. 26, 1942, Trevor-Roper, p. 339; entry for July 26, 1942, Gerhard Ritter (ed.), *Hitlers Tischgespräche im Führerhauptquartier 1941-1942* (Bonn: Athenäum-Verlag, 1951), pp. 123 f.

119. Entry for Feb. 22, 1942, Trevor-Roper, p. 328; entry for April 25, 1942, *ibid.*, p. 442 and Ritter p. 78.

120. Entry for Sept. 5, 1942, Trevor-Roper, p. 691.

121. OKW/Ausl VII, "Koloniale Unterrichtung Nr. 15," Sept. 23, 1941, T-77/643/1838786.

122. OKW/Ausl VII, "Koloniale Unterrichtung Nr. 16," Nov. 20, 1941, ibid., frames 1838779-782.

contemporary efforts of the OKW to coordinate the preparation of appropriate equipment types for colonial employment, partly on the basis of experience in North Africa.

Colonel Geldern had returned from a tour of three months in the North African campaign in July 1941 and began the dissemination of his experiences relevant to general colonial questions soon thereafter. On the political side, he stressed that the officers and men of the German Africa-Corps were disappointed by what they were seeing of Africa—hardly a surprising development—and were not likely to become imbued with colonial enthusiasm. This underlined the need to emphasize the differences between the deserts of Cyrenaica and the proposed central African empire flowing, if not with milk and honey, at least with cocoa and vegetable oil. Of more immediate concern were Geldern's deductions about tactics and equipment; these were disseminated to the interested agencies beginning with July 25, 1941, and continuing in installments thereafter.[123] The Colonial Regulations for the Armed Forces continued to be the subject of discussion and redrafting,[124] and new maps of Africa were ready for distribution.[125] The last report on African experiences in connection with future colonial activities and on the gamut of technical colonial preparations was sent out by Geldern on December 18, 1941.[126] At this time, the German army was suffering its decisive defeat on the Russian front, and the forty-seven German military agencies on the mailing list presumably

123. OKW/Ausl VII, "Koloniale Unterrichtung Nr. 12," July 24, 1941, ibid., frames 1838808-811 and Nr. 13 of Aug. 4, 1941, frames 1838802-807.

124. Ibid., frame 1838811. The latest recorded contribution located to date is a suggested one for OKW/AWA/W Wiss, of April 23, 1942, T-77/642/1838501-502.

125. OKW/Ausl VII, "Koloniale Unterrichtung Nr. 14," Aug. 27, 1941, T-77/643/1838191-192. See also Reichswirtschaftsministerium, "V So 1971/41 Betr. Koloniale Vorbereitungsarbeiten," Oct. 31, 1941, T-77/642/1838592.

126. OKW/Ausl VII, "Koloniale Unterrichtung Nr. 17," Dec. 18, 1941, T-77/643/1838773-776. Since there are documents of a later date in the same and related folders, but the collection of Koloniale Unterrichtungen ends with No. 17, it may be assumed that no further issues appeared.

had more urgent matters to attend to. The Colonial Policy Office of the Party also had to reorient its perspective. In 1942 the special series of studies on colonial policy, heralded in August of 1940, began to appear; but the new titles announced in February 1942 bore little resemblance to the confidently planned handbooks for German colonial administrators. From future German colonial policy and practice, the focus had shifted to historical and bibliographic themes: "The Bases of British World Rule," "Experiences in My Years of Travel in the Colonies," and "Colonial Literature in Germany."[127] Colonial activity in the last years of National Socialism thus returned to its character in the first years; that of propagandizing for the "colonial idea" by books and pamphlets without reference to the conduct of policy or the realities of the world situation.[128]

VIII.

It is now possible to put the colonial question into the general context of the history of Hitler's Germany, at least in a preliminary way. In the two years preceding the outbreak of World War II, Hitler for the first time gave real indications of a willingness to place German power behind the vocal aspirations of the colonialists. Thinking in terms of political concessions wrung from the other powers, Hitler wanted preparations started for occupying and administering a recovered African empire. The outbreak of war at first pushed the colonial question into the background, but the course of the fighting automatically

127. *Deutscher Kolonial-Dienst,* VII (Feb. 1942) No. 1/2, p. 28. For the planned titles, see n. 71 above. The actual titles: No. 1: Paul Ritter, "Lebensgrundlagen britischer Weltherrschaft," No. 2: Rudolf Asmis, "Erfahrungen aus meinen kolonialen Wanderjahren," No. 3: "Koloniales Schrifttum in Deutschland." It should be noted, however, that the only one of these seen by the author (No. 2) carries a 1941 copyright.

128. The author's copy of Ernst Kienitz, *Zeittafel zur deutschen Kolonialgeschichte* (Munich: Fichte-Verlag, 1941) contains a forwarding circular to the addressee—a German teachers' library—from the Abteilung Schrifttum of the Reichskolonialbund of April 29, 1943. Many other items are listed in the *NS-Bibliographie.*

brought it back into prominence in the summer of 1940. The eager hopes of June and July became entangled with the indecisive tergiversations of German diplomacy as Hitler tried to reconcile German, Italian, and Spanish colonial hopes with what appeared to be the possibilities of the moment. It may well seem to some that, just as in other accounts the colonial issue has been slighted, so here its role has been exaggerated. Nevertheless, the evidence does show that in the summer and fall of 1940 Hitler's colonial ideas had crystallized to the point where the central African empire with its appendages in Southwest Africa and on or off the coast of Morocco was a significant factor in his political and military policy. The German initiative of the summer of 1940, frittered away in the fall, was lost in the winter due to Italy's disasters in the Balkans and North Africa. A variety of factors outside the scope of this study kept Germany from regaining the initiative in the Mediterranean through an agreement with France in the spring of 1941; thereafter the attack on Russia would first make the African colonies look less valuable by comparison and then unattainable by defeat.

All the elaborate discussion of racial problems and jurisdictional issues and all the technical preparations were in vain. The tie between German territorial aspirations for settlement in the East and for raw materials in Africa proved real only in the sense that neither could be secured. The Germans would have to settle for less territory than ever and buy many of their raw materials as before. Whether in this they were as unfortunate as the colonial enthusiasts in World War II Germany believed, is at least open to question. The ship of African colonialism was already sinking when Hitler tried to get aboard. Most others have since abandoned it, and only a few at the southern end of the continent appear to prefer drowning. Defeat in World War II saved Germany from the agonies of this choice.

July 20, 1944: The Plot to Kill Hitler

It is a little more than twenty-five years back to D-Day, the invasion of Western Europe on June 6, 1944. Two days before, in the south, the Allies had taken Rome; two weeks later, the great Soviet offensive tore open Germany's Eastern Front. Those coördinated attacks would squeeze the life out of Hitler's empire. But for a moment, it looked as if the war might end much more quickly. On July 20, 1944, a bomb exploded in Hitler's headquarters, a few feet from the dictator himself, and a broadly based opposition attempted, primarily in Berlin and Paris, to take power away from the Nazis and reestablish decency inside and peace outside Germany. But the explosion did not kill Hitler, and the attempted coup was quickly and successfully throttled. The war ground on. What had happened?

Opposition to the government of a totalitarian police state is no easy matter. If you make your disapproval of the government's policies known, you do not appear on the eleven o'clock TV screen, you disappear forever. And you disappear quietly—only a few friends and relatives learn that you are not around anymore; the controlled mass media make no reference to the event, unless the government itself decides to use the matter in a context of its own choosing—with no provision of equal time for the inmate of camp or tomb. The same media will have broadcast an almost impenetrable fog of propaganda in the first place, making everyone incredulous of any who have seen

This essay was originally a talk given in July 1969 at Colorado State University, Fort Collins, Colorado, to commemorate the twenty-fifth anniversary of the plot of July 20, 1944. A slightly different text was published in the *Michigan Quarterly Review,* 10, No. 2 (Spring 1971), pp. 125-30. It is reprinted here by permission of the *Michigan Quarterly Review.*

some light and who try to persuade others that they are indeed in a fog. As in the parable of Plato, the prisoners still chained in the cave who have seen only the passing shadows assume *them* to be reality, rejecting as preposterous and unreal the visions of those who have left the cave to look at the world in the light of truth.

Nevertheless, overthrowing a totalitarian regime is not impossible. As in East Germany in June 1953 and in Hungary in October 1956 sufficient mass dissatisfaction can topple an unpopular police state from below. In both those cases, only outside military intervention could reinstate a tottering tyranny. Obviously, no outside power would ever have saved Hitler as the Red Army saved Walter Ulbricht and Janos Kadar. The German people's massive support of Hitler closed this road, however, in Nazi Germany. A successor government might have secured mass support by dispelling the fog and revealing the Third Reich in all its hideous reality, but this presupposes a thoroughly successful coup that could change the role of the mass media. The National Socialist regime, which was popular in peacetime, became, if not more popular, certainly less vulnerable in the early years of World War II when Germany's spectacular victories combined with the pressures of wartime to consolidate the population behind its rulers.

If the government could not be toppled from below, then the only alternative was from above, that is, from the inside. Individuals in important positions within the government might, precisely because of their positions, gain greater insight into the true nature of the regime. They might then try to persuade other officials of their insight and, joining with sympathetic individuals outside the government, attempt to seize power from within the governmental structure. The opposition in Germany necessarily took this direction. But note the moral dilemma. If you quit your position, you could disclaim any connection with the policies you opposed—but you would give up any chance to help in a major and active way in the effort to topple the regime. If you remained in office to stay close to the levers of power for the day of decision, you would have to participate in a regime you believed to be evil. Such a dilemma is necessarily most difficult for precisely those most sensitive to moral questions.

A few such people were in the German government, their numbers varying, their views differing, and their motives not always pure—nor therefore entirely opportunistic either. Some came to be horrified at the excesses that accompanied victories; others, to be appalled at the unwillingness to react constructively to the onrush of defeat. Different straws break the backs of different camels: Carl Goerdeler, the mayor of Leipzig, quit when the Party removed the statue of the great composer Mendelssohn from the city square; Helmuth Stieff, the chief of "Organization" for the Germany army general staff, when atrocities in Poland and Russia made him, as he wrote his wife, ashamed to be a German.[1] Diplomats and generals, labor leaders and clergymen, politicians of the old parties and disillusioned National Socialists, formed a loose association of kindred spirits about whom we know a good deal, but not as much as we might like, because conspiracies in a police state do not keep extensive files (and much of the little they kept was destroyed).

Ludwig Beck, for instance, had been chief of staff of the German army since 1934. He objected vehemently to suggestions of aggressive war in 1935; he became increasingly alarmed at the reckless drive toward war, and at certain domestic policies. Opposed to attacking Germany's neighbors, Beck attempted to rally the other German generals for a united opposition, a sort of general strike of the generals, against what he considered a foolhardy, danger-

1. Helmuth Stieff to his wife, Nov. 21, 1939, in Hans Rothfels (ed.), "Ausgewählte Briefe von Generalmajor Helmuth Stieff," *Vierteljahrshefte für Zeitgeschichte*, 2, No. 3 (July 1954), p. 300.

ous, and immoral policy. He felt that a military man in a high position cannot restrict himself to purely technical details in the face of an imminent disaster, clearly perceived. Unable to move the commander in chief or other senior generals to a collective stand against Hitler, he resigned and worked with others in the opposition. Beck gave some of his key papers, warnings against the policies of Hitler, to an associate who had helped him draft some of them; many were destroyed in the war, but some survive to enable us to trace his views.

Julius Leber was a socialist from Lübeck, a labor leader who had worked hard to infuse some life and enthusiasm into German democracy in the Weimar years. When the Nazis attempted to murder him in the night after Hitler's appointment as chancellor, he was arrested, released, and arrested again, and spent four years in a concentration camp. After his release, although under constant surveillance, he did his best to keep in touch with like-minded men among former trade unionists. He was, in effect, the opposition's intermediary between labor and some generals, and many of both groups looked to him for a key role in any post-Hitler Germany.

Ulrich von Hassell, a professional diplomat, had served as ambassador to Italy in the 1930's. Hitler's dangerous foreign policy alarmed him, a conservative nationalist. The trend toward an alliance between Germany and Italy worried him as much as the hostility of prior years—either seemed dangerous. Dismissed in 1938, von Hassell could only observe the trend to disaster, but he made contact with other opponents, tried to recruit additional ones, and kept a diary that survived his arrest and execution to become one of our most important firsthand sources for the history of the opposition to Hitler.[2]

Since in National Socialist Germany only organized in-

2. Ulrich von Hassell, *Vom Andern Deutschland* (Zurich: Atlantis, 1946).

siders could hope to overthrow the regime, my account must set aside the many ordinary people from all walks of life who refused to conform, who helped the persecuted, who passed on news they had heard on forbidden radio stations, with high moral courage. But sporadic individual acts of defiance, however heroic, could count for little.

The only possible exception to this generalization would be an attempted assassination; and it was precisely such an attempt in November 1939, planned for many months by the individual who carried it out and paid for it with his life, that almost worked. But even that project, though very intelligently conceived and executed, could look only to Hitler's death, not to the establishment of anything differently structured threafter.[3] Any effort that was to include a seizure of power and not only the removal of Hitler necessarily called for planning by insiders.

The opposition at first tried to get the highest men in the army to use their authority against the regime. But the obtuseness of the first, and the weakness of the second commander in chief blocked all prospects of success along this route. When Hitler himself assumed command of the army in December 1941 assassination followed by seizure of control seemed the only possible avenue. With Hitler removed, the doubters would rally to the determined among the military, and together they would overawe, or crush, those still loyal to the swastika. But such a scheme was immensely difficult.

The first problem was finding someone with access to Hitler willing to try to kill him. Most of those around Hitler were personal friends. If any were doubters, finding them out was not easy. You could not take a poll. Furthermore, Hitler himself took increasing precautions against assassination, changing his schedule, declining visits near the front, and increasing his escort. In March 1943 the

3. Lothar Gruchmann (ed.), *Autobiographie eines Attentäters, Johann Georg Elser* (Stuttgart: Deutsche Verlags-Anstalt, 1970).

conspirators put a bomb on Hitler's plane, but the detonator failed, leaving the conspirators the ticklish task of recovering the unexploded bomb. One conspirator planned to blow himself up right next to Hitler—and then had to disconnect his own fuse when the Fuehrer left before the device was timed to explode. Other schemes came to naught for different reasons. And some of the conspirators had doubts. As long as Hitler was winning, an assassination followed by defeat in war would lead to another stab-in-the-back legend among the German people—not a very firm basis for creating a democratic order. Once Hitler was losing, on the other hand, a coup would look to the outside world like a last minute attempt to avert the consequences of defeat. Furthermore, what could then be saved anyway?

After the invasion of Normandy, the problem became acute. Should they go ahead? One of the key conspirators answered:

> The assassination must be attempted, at any cost. Even should that fail, the attempt to seize power in the capital must be undertaken. We must prove to the world and to future generations that the men of the German Resistance movement dared to take the decisive step and to hazard their lives upon it. Compared with this object, nothing else matters.[4]

Plans to seize power in the capital at the assassination were, of course, essential. These plans were developed in the Replacement Army under the cover of contingency planning to cope with any revolt by foreign workers inside Germany or commando raids. This plan, called "Valkyrie," was partly regularized and deposited in sealed envelopes in all military district headquarters—to be opened only when the code word was given—and was partly to be supplemented by secret additions calling for a complete takeover.

In World War I, Germany had transferred executive

4. Henning von Tresckow quoted in Fabian von Schlabrendorff, *They Almost Killed Hitler,* ed. Gero v. S. Gaevernitz (New York: Macmillan, 1947), p. 103.

and police powers to the military districts covering all Germany. In each district, the local military leader gave orders to civilian as well as military agencies. In World War II, Hitler refused to allow this; the Party and the police remained superior. But "Valkyrie" planned to transfer executive power to the military, along with authority to mobilize all reserves, thereby enabling them to dominate the situation when the active units were at the front. With a concept familiar to the German public and military from the previous war, this plan offered real promise. And it could be formulated without arousing suspicion.

Separate plans were made to seize radio and telegraph facilities, to initiate local liaison officers into at least parts of the plot, and to explain to the German people and army what was going on. Utmost secrecy was, of course, imperative. Claus von Stauffenberg, a man who combined remarkable ability with decisiveness, played an increasingly important part in this planning. With some conspirators arrested and others hesitating, he infused energy into the group and recruited additional men. His organizational talents simultaneously assured him a key part in the conspiracy, and earned him the post of chief of staff of the Replacement Army, a position that gave him access to the Fuehrer's headquarters. Though he had lost one eye, one hand, and three fingers of the other hand in the war, Stauffenberg had become the motor of the conspiracy.

After several postponements, the conspirators decided on the conference of July 20, 1944, which Stauffenberg would attend, as the occasion for their attempt. Stauffenberg flew to East Prussia, placed his briefcase with the bomb under the table around which Hitler and his military advisers gathered, left the meeting on a pretext, saw the explosion, which he assumed had killed Hitler, bluffed his way out of the headquarters, and flew back to Berlin. There and in Paris—where conspirators held key posts—the coup was attempted. In Berlin, the conspirators received the special signal and gathered at the Ministry of War; the codeword for implementing "Valkyrie" went out to all military district headquarters, and orders to seize power went out over the teleprinter. In Paris, the military actually seized power and arrested top police officials. But Hitler had not been killed.

By an extraordinary mischance, the explosion that wounded and killed several left Hitler with only minor injuries. His headquarters in East Prussia immediately inaugurated counter measures. The intended blocking of telephone and telegraph circuits could not be maintained, because Hitler had not been killed, and counter orders from East Prussia crossed those of "Valkyrie" from Berlin. The conspirators could not go back—and did not want to in any case. They tried to move on with their scheme, sending out their orders and proclamations, hoping to take over power in spite of Hitler's survival. In a few hours, the bulk of Germany's military leaders made their choice. As between a still living Hitler and his opponents, they sided with the dictator. In those few hours, the uprising was crushed, the most immediately implicated conspirators summarily shot, and the authority of the regime firmly reasserted. In the evening Hitler spoke over the radio from East Prussia to reassure the people that he was still alive, obviously destined by fate to continue to lead them. And continue to lead them he did, to death and destruction for added millions.

The failure of the coup, in fact, left the National Socialist leadership in a stronger position than ever. The Gestapo had not fully understood the conspiracy; they knew something of it, but had been kept from picking up all of the conspirators by Himmler's own doubts about the outcome of the war. Now that most of the opposition had necessarily revealed themselves in the events of July 20, or by association with the conspirators or from seized records, a great haul of oppositionists was taken to jail and to the scaffold, while others previously arrested were now dealt with more harshly. As the war ground on along the shrinking fringes of Hitler's empire, hundreds were executed inside it for their real or suspected involvement in the conspiracy. Some were tried and then executed, some were simply murdered, still others committed suicide lest they endanger others under torture. Thus Hitler's control tightened, as the skeptical and the critical disappeared together and the atmosphere of terror intensified. He could now radically increase the power of the police at the expense of the army, and strengthen the Party at the expense of the army and the administration.

As Hitler's first triumph had been his assumption of power in 1933, so his last triumph was the maintenance of that power against internal enemies. A few of these were not discovered right away, and a few were never discovered at all, but no significant internal challenge to the Fuehrer's power remained. He had not been overthrown either from below or from above; he could now be removed only by the armed might of the great anti-German coalition he himself had forged.

But, in spite of the continuing war, in spite of the increased Nazification of German life, in spite of failure, the events of that summer day remain significant for Germany and for world history. The Germans are the most numerous and potentially most powerful people in Europe after the Russians; whatever significantly affects them has important implications for the continent as a whole. The dramatic success of West Germany's physical reconstruction has obscured her far more difficult psychological reconstruction. If the German people—three-fourths of them in West Germany—are to find an integral place in Europe and their self-respect, they need a past to which they can relate positively. As the various European nationalities emerged from non-national constructions in the nineteenth century, and as other nations have emerged out of the colonial empires in the twentieth, one distinguishing feature of that process has been the effort to relate the present to the past, to give independence a dimension in time, and to provide in difficult struggles the self-confidence and hope that comes from perceiving past struggles and accomplishments. The current pleas for Black History simply illustrate the point. After 1945, with its total debacle, and with revelations of greater horrors than the most determined foes of Hitler had even imagined, Germany desperately needed the signposts, the examples, the heroes, and the traditions to which a new Germany might hark back and relate in the future. Here the conspiracy against Hitler is of central importance.

Not perfect men and women making perfect decisions, but fallible people facing hard choices and cruel alternatives, the members of the resistance provide a basis for a post-Nazi order and point to a future in which new issues can be measured by a standard of decency. In an age without heroes, in a country where the heroes have been too often those willing to sacrifice the spirit of man to the power of the state, a group that tried to assert the opposite—that the state must be subordinated to elemental rights—stands forth as a standard to which people can adhere and by which they can judge.

By no means all Germans have found this standard acceptable. In fact, the willingness or reluctance to do so may provide a touchstone by which most modern Germans can easily be assessed. Many have tried to avoid the Twentieth of July in uneasy distaste; many have condemned as traitors the very men who sacrificed their lives to save Germany from Hitler's frenzy of destruction. As the picture of the opposition, its hopes, plans, and aspirations has become clearer, many have looked to it positively as representative of values that have meaning for all men, and as symbolizing a tradition that deserves a central place in a new beginning for their country, a country that desperately needs a new beginning.

This is important for Germany's relations with other peoples as well. Hitler's tyranny had to be terminated by the exertions and sacrifices of others. But the others now know that inside Germany some men and women tried to end the tyranny themselves, at the risk of everything, and at the price of their lives. Thus, the dead of the resistance, though sorely missed in postwar Germany, have given it one of its most important assets.

There is, in addition, a point in all this for everyone. The judge who presided over the sham trials of the conspirators, Roland Freisler, was killed when a bomb fell on the People's Court. But sham trials did not end with Freisler's death, and tyranny did not end with Hitler's. A quarter of a century later, the example of those who dared defy the tyrant is surely still worthy of remembrance.

When I became responsible for microfilming the captured German records kept in this country before their return to Germany, I was also responsible for assigning very personal records to the "privileged" category. One of the first films we wanted to make public was that of the Gestapo reports to Hitler on their investigation into the Twentieth of July. But the last letters of some of the conspirators were attached to the reports. Certainly nothing could be more personal than the last letters to his wife, his mother, or his children of a man about to be executed; but it seemed to me that an exception to "privilege" could properly be made so that the men of the resistance, not the Gestapo, would have the last word. The American army authorities were fortunately persuaded by this consideration—a judgment ironically confirmed when a neo-Nazi publication of the police reports carefully omitted every one of the letters.

One of the conspirators wrote to his mother before his execution on August 8, 1944:

> At the end of a life greatly blessed with love and friendship, I have only gratitude toward God and humility before His

will. I greatly regret causing you this sorrow after all the sad things that you have lived through. I ask you to forgive me for this. I have had more than two weeks to place my life and my actions before God, and I am convinced that I will find him a merciful judge. The extent of the internal conflict faced in recent years by men like myself is simply incomprehensible to those who are secure in their belief [in National Socialism] which I simply do not share. I can assure you that no ambitious seeking for power motivated my actions. My actions were motivated only by my patriotic feelings, the concern for Germany as it has developed over two millennia, and the worry over its internal and external development. Therefore I stand unashamed before my ancestors, my father, and my brothers. Perhaps a time will come when people will arrive at a different evaluation of our conduct, when we will be considered not bums but warners and patriots. I pray that the wonderful way in which we have been called will serve to honor God.[5]

5. Count Peter Yorck von Wartenburg to his mother, Erich Zimmermann and Hans-Adolf Jacobsen (eds.), *20. Juli 1944* (Bonn: Berto-Verlag, 1960), p. 252.

For additional details, and an extensive bibliography, see Peter Hoffmann, *The History of the German Resistance, 1933-1945*, trans. by Richard Barry (Cambridge, Mass.: MIT Press, 1977).

Bibliography

The publications dealing with World War II are so numerous that any comprehensive bibliography, even if restricted to Western languages, would fill volumes. The suggestions listed here provide an introduction to the subject and should facilitate further reading. The selection and the comments are necessarily arbitrary. The emphasis has been on English language works (or translations into English); and many of the books listed provide bibliographies of their own, often in considerable detail and in some instances with commentary.

Anyone interested in locating works on the war or any aspect of it should start with Janet Ziegler's, *World War II: Books in English, 1945-65* (Stanford, Calif.: Hoover Institution Press, 1971) and will want to urge the author to bring this invaluable work up to date. Current bibliographic coverage of publications in English as well as other languages is most conveniently found in the French journal, *Revue d'histoire de la deuxième guerre mondiale,* and in the annual *Jahresbibliographie* volumes issued by the Bibliothek für Zeitgeschichte in Stuttgart. The holocaust and war crimes trials are covered by Jacob Robinson and Philip Friedman, *Guide to Jewish History under Nazi Impact* (New York: Yivo and Yad Washem, 1960); additional specialized bibliographies are listed by Ziegler.

A fine military history of the whole war is Martha Byrd Hoyle's *A World in Flames: A History of World War II* (New York: Atheneum, 1970), while its diplomacy is covered by John L. Snell's *Illusion and Necessity: The Diplomacy of Global War 1939-1945* (Boston: Houghton Mifflin, 1963). The most useful cartographic coverage of the war is in volume 2 of Vincent J. Esposito (ed.), *The West Point Atlas of American Wars* (New York: Praeger, 1959). The survey by Gordon Wright, *The Ordeal of Total War* (New York: Harper & Row, 1968), is confined to the European side of the conflict; there is as yet nothing like it for the East Asian war. Until one appears,

F. C. Jones, *Japan's New Order in East Asia: Its Rise and Fall, 1937-45* (London, New York: Oxford University Press, 1954), Ienaga Saburo, *The Pacific War, 1931-1945* (New York: Pantheon Books, 1978), and Christopher Thorne, *Allies of a Kind: The United States, Britain, and the War against Japan, 1941-1945* (London, New York: Oxford University Press, 1978) may be used. The volumes in the *Survey of International Affairs* series issued by the Royal Institute of International Affairs are extremely helpful, even though they were written much earlier than many of the monographs otherwise listed in this bibliography.

Those who want a general idea of the resources available for research on World War II, or who plan to do such work themselves, will begin with the papers published in Robert Wolfe (ed.), *Captured German and Related Records* (Athens, Ohio: Ohio University Press, 1974), and in James E. O'Neill and Robert W. Krauskopf (eds.), *World War II: An Account of Its Documents* (Washington, D.C.: Howard University Press, 1976). They will also examine *The Second World War: A Guide to Documents in the Public Record Office* (London: H.M. Stationery Office, 1972), and Howard M. Smyth's *Secrets of the Fascist Era* (Carbondale, Ill.: Southern Illinois University Press, 1975). The suggestions for further reading which follow contain results of important research already accomplished.

The official histories of World War II are voluminous, and in many cases they are extremely well written. The British set, which is divided into military, civilian, and medical series, is almost completed. Of particular interest for their broad coverage are the volumes entitled *Grand Strategy* by J. R. M. Butler and others, *The War at Sea* by Stephen R. Roskill, *The Strategic Air Offensive* by Sir Charles Webster and Noble Frankland, and *British Foreign Policy in the Second World War* by Sir Llewellyn Woodward. Unfortunately the volumes were, for the most part, printed without footnotes on the ridiculous assumption that all readers can easily use the documented versions in London when the records cited have been opened to research!

The American series are separated by service. Samuel Eliot

Morison has given his own inimitable touch to the fifteen-volume *History of United States Naval Operations in World War II* (Boston: Little, Brown, 1947-62). Wesley F. Craven and James L. Cate sign for the seven volumes on *The Army Air Forces in World War II* (Chicago: University of Chicago Press, 1948-58). The Marine Corps issued two series of campaign histories, one preliminary and one more detailed, but the general reader would do best to begin with Jeter A. Isely and Philip A. Crowl, *The U.S. Marines and Amphibious War: Its Theory and Practice in the Pacific* (Princeton, N.J.: Princeton University Press, 1951).

The American army's *U.S. Army in World War II* is made up of several series in which many excellent works are indispensable for anyone seriously interested in either the broader strategy or the specific operations of World War II, and which include extensive and often exceedingly helpful material on the Germans and Japanese as well. The volumes of Maurice Matloff and Edwin M. Snell on *Strategic Planning for Coalition Warfare* and by Richard M. Leighton and Robert W. Coakley on *Global Logistics and Strategy* are espescially important; others are essential for understanding campaigns in which American forces were engaged, from *Victory in Papua* by Samuel F. Milner to *Cross-Channel Attack* by Gordon A. Harrison. Additional volumes from this set have been mentioned in notes or are listed in this bibliography. All the American works are carefully footnoted so that the reader can retrace the research and ask for the declassification of specific documents where this is necessary.

The Soviet Union's six-volume official history, *Istoriya Velikoy Otchestvennoy Voyni Sovetskogo Soyuze 1941-1945* [History of the Great Patriotic War of the Soviet Union 1941-1945], was published in 1960-63. Prepared by a group of authors collectively, it covers economic and political as well as military events. A German but no English language translation has appeared.[1] The footnotes are scanty and unrevealing,

1. The German edition was prepared by East German scholars and published by the German Democratic Republic's Militärverlag under the title *Geschichte des Grossen Vaterländischen Krieges der Sowjetunion*. There is something like a one-volume English language Soviet condensation: *Great*

but the information in these volumes is useful all the same. The problems of working on the war on the Eastern front and using Russian materials are described in the books by Erickson and Ziemke listed subsequently.

A West German history is now being issued in ten volumes by the Militärgeschichtliche Forschungsamt in Freiburg under the title *Das Deutsche Reich und der Zweite Weltkrieg*. Critical comments suggest that those unable to read the official Japanese history are not missing much;[2] there is something of a substitute in the works prepared for the Americans by Japanese after the war and recently edited by Donald S. Detwiler and Charles B. Burdick for Garland Publishing, Inc. There are also official series issued by other belligerents: Canada, Italy, India, Australia, China,[3] Holland, Yugoslavia, and Norway, to name just a sample, but these are all of more limited interest or in languages used by few Americans.[4]

Books on the war which deal with broad strategic issues by German scholars are Andreas Hillgruber's very informative *Hitlers Strategie: Politik und Kriegführung, 1940-1941* (Frankfurt am Main: Bernard & Graefe, 1965), Hans-Adolf Jacobsen's suggestive *Zur Konzeption einer Geschichte des Zweiten Weltkrieges 1939-1945* (Frankfurt am Main: Bernard & Graefe, 1964), and Jochen Thies's illuminating book on Hitler's objectives, *Architekt der Weltherrschaft: Die "Endziele" Hitlers* (Düsseldorf: Droste, 1976). Helpful in spite of some doubtful

---

Patriotic War of the Soviet Union 1941-1945, A General Outline (Moscow: Progress Publishers, 1974). In 1971 the Soviet Union began publication of a new official history, *Istoriya Vtoroy Mirovoi Voina 1939-1945* [History of the Second World War, 1939-1945], in twelve volumes. This set is also being published by the German Democratic Republic's military publishing house as *Geschichte des Zweiten Weltkrieges, 1939-1945;* the last volumes of the twelve have not appeared as yet.

2. Tsunoda Jun, "Die amtliche japanische Kriegsgeschichtsschreibung über den Zweiten Weltkrieg in Ostasien und im Pazifik," *Jahresbibliographie 1973*, pp. 393-405.

3. There is a one-volume English language summary of the 100-volume official history of the Republic of China; *History of the Sino-Japanese War (1937-1945)* (Taipei, Taiwan: Chung Wu Publishing Co., 1971).

4. A survey of the various programs which, though dated, is still helpful by Johann C. Allmayer-Beck, "Die internationale amtliche Kriegsgeschichtsschreibung über den Zweiten Weltkrieg," *Jahresbibliographie 1962*, pp. 507-40.

interpretations in the first volume is Michael Salewski's three-volume work, *Die deutsche Seekriegsleitung, 1935-1945* (Frankfurt am Main: Bernard & Graefe, 1970-75). Essential reading for Germany's role in the war is Norman Rich's two-volume analysis, *Hitler's War Aims* (New York: Norton, 1973-74). From the British side, Winston S. Churchill's great work, *The Second World War,* 6 vols. (Boston: Houghton Mifflin, 1948-53), combines memoir, analysis, and documentation in a synthesis that commands admiration even as it requires correction.

The early disasters of the Allies in the West are handled well in Brian Bond, *France and Belgium, 1939-1940* (London: Davis-Poynter, 1975); the French archives were utilized by Jeffry A. Gunsburg for his *Divided and Conquered: The French High Command and the Defeat of the West, 1940* (Westport, Conn.: Greenwood Press, 1979); Vichy France is covered elegantly by Robert O. Paxton, *Vichy France: Old Guard and New Order* (New York: Alfred A. Knopf, 1972); and the French collaborators receive more careful coverage than they deserve from Bertram M. Gordon, *Collaborationism in France During the Second World War* (Ithaca, N.Y.: Cornell University Press, 1980). The Scandinavian theater is best introduced by Earl F. Ziemke's *The German Northern Theater of Operations, 1940-1945* (Dept. of the Army Pamphlet 20-271; Washington, D.C.: Government Printing Office, 1960).

Affairs in the Balkans are the subject of an endless literature in which Martin L. Van Creveld, *Hitler's Strategy 1940-1941: The Balkan Clue* (London: Cambridge University Press, 1973), Carlyle A. Macartney, *October Fifteenth: A History of Modern Hungary,* 2 vols. (Edinburgh: University Press, 1956), Andreas Hillgruber, *Hitler, König Carol und Marschall Antonescu: Die deutsch-rumänischen Beziehungen 1938-1944* (Wiesbaden: Steiner, 1954), Philippe Marguerat, *Le IIIe Reich et le pétrole roumain, 1938-1940* (Geneva: A. W. Sijthoff, 1977), Hans-Joachim Hoppe, *Bulgarien—Hitlers eigenwilliger Verbündete* (Stuttgart: Deutsche Verlags-Anstalt, 1979), Walter A. Roberts, *Tito, Mihailović and the Allies, 1941-1945* (New Brunswick, N.J.: Rutgers University Press, 1973), and Jürgen Förster, *Stalingrad: Risse im Bündnis 1942/43* (Freiburg: Rombach, 1975) provide a good introduction. A solid and dependable account of the war in Poland in 1939 remains to be written; until it is, Nicholas Bethell, *The War Hitler Won: The Fall of Poland, September 1939* (New York: Holt, Rinehart and Winston, 1972), will have to do. International developments about Poland are the subject of an extensive literature: Vojtech Mastny, *Russia's Road to the Cold War* (New York: Columbia University Press, 1979) and Richard C. Lukas, *The Strange Allies: The United States and Poland, 1941-1945* (Knoxville: University of Tennessee Press, 1978) may serve as starting points.

The war on the Eastern front, as already mentioned, presents some very special and serious problems. Of great help is John Erickson, *The Soviet High Command* (London: Macmillan, 1962). The same author's *The Road to Stalingrad: Stalin's War with Germany*, vol. 1 (New York: Harper & Row, 1975), is filled with interesting details but very difficult to follow, especially in the absence of maps. Earl F. Ziemke's *Stalingrad to Berlin: The German Defeat in the East* (Washington, D.C.: Government Printing Office, 1968), is the best general work for the years 1942-45; Albert Seaton, *The Russo-German War 1941-45* (London: Arthur Barker, 1971), deals with the military history of the whole campaign; Seweryn Bialer's edition of excerpts from Soviet memoirs, *Stalin and His Generals* (London: Souvenir Press, 1970), offers the best introduction to the Soviet side of the war; John A. Armstrong and others, *Soviet Partisans in World War II* (Madison: University of Wisconsin Press, 1964), covers the problem of partisan warfare; Christian Streit, *Keine Kameraden: Die Wehrmacht und die sowjetischen Kriegsgefangenen, 1941-1945* (Stuttgart: Deutsche Verlags-Anstalt, 1978), handles the terrible fate of the five million Soviet prisoners of war; while Charles W. Sydnor, Jr., *Soldiers of Destruction: The SS Death's Head Division, 1933-1945* (Princeton, N.J.: Princeton University Press, 1977) and Helmut Krausnick, *Die Truppe des Weltanschauungskrieges: Die Einsatzgruppen der Sicherheitspolizei und des SD, 1938-1942* (Stuttgart: Deutsche Verlags-Anstalt, 1980) provide insight into the new types of murderous organizations established by the Germans.

Italy's role in the war is handled in the English language in the British and American official histories, by Michael Howard, *The Mediterranean Strategy in the Second World War* (London: Weidenfeld & Nicolson, 1968), and by Frederick W. Deakin, *The Brutal Friendship: Mussolini, Hitler, and the Fall of Italian Fascism* (New York: Harper & Row, 1962); the circumstances surrounding her exit are dealt with by Josef Schröder, *Italiens Kriegsaustritt 1943* (Göttingen: Musterschmidt, 1969). Spain's role is the subject of Charles B. Burdick, *Germany's Military Strategy and Spain in World War II* (Syracuse, N.Y.: University of Syracuse Press, 1968), and Donald S. Detwiler, *Hitler, Franco und Gibraltar: Die Frage des spanischen Eintritts in den Zweiten Weltkrieg* (Wiesbaden: Steiner, 1962). The internal situation in German-controlled Europe is dealt with by volumes in the series of the Royal Institute of International Affairs, the second volume of Norman Rich's book listed above, a number of books by Alan Milward, and the reports of the United States Strategic Bombing Survey.

The role of the United States is covered effectively by the official histories. A good introduction to American diplomacy is provided by Robert Dallek, *Franklin D. Roosevelt and American Foreign Policy, 1932-1945* (New York: Oxford University Press, 1979), while the whole range of America's role is best followed in the second and third volumes of Forrest C. Pogue's thoughtful and well-written biography *George C. Marshall, Ordeal and Hope, 1939-1942,* and *Organizer of Victory, 1943-1945* (New York: Viking, 1965, 1973).

For relations among the Allies, William H. McNeill's volume *America, Britain, and Russia: Their Co-operation and Conflict, 1941-1946,* originally published in 1953 in the Royal Institute of International Affairs series and reprinted in 1970 (New York and London: Johnson Reprint), remains helpful, while the books of the two revisionist schools illuminate American attitudes of the period in which they were written—1948-52 and 1965-75—rather than the events they purport to describe. James R. Leutze's *Bargaining for Supremacy: Anglo-American Naval Collaboration, 1937-1941* (Chapel Hill: University of North Carolina Press, 1977), George C. Herring, Jr., *Aid to Russia, 1941-1946* (New York: Columbia University Press, 1973), and George V. Kecewicz, *Great Britain, the Soviet*

Union, and the Polish Government in Exile (1939-45) (The Hague: Nijhoff, 1979), open new ways to examine the alliance against Hitler. On the Axis side, Bernd Martin, *Deutschland und Japan im Zweiten Weltkrieg* (Göttingen: Musterschmidt, 1969), and Johanna M. Meskill, *Hitler and Japan: The Hollow Alliance* (New York: Atherton, 1966), provide a good place to begin.

This brings us to the war in East Asia on which the literature is not nearly as extensive as on the European aspect. Louis Morton's *The War in the Pacific: Strategy and Command, The First Two Years* in the army's official history surveys a substantial portion of the conflict. The Japanese studies edited by Detwiler and Burdick have already been mentioned. An English translation of Hattori Takushiro's four-volume *Complete History of the Greater East Asia War* is available at the United States Army's Center for Military History. Of the Japanese books published in English translation perhaps the most useful are Fushida Mitsuo and Okumiya Masatake, *Midway: The Battle that Doomed Japan* (Annapolis: Naval Institute Press, 1955), which covers far more than the title suggests, and Hayashi Saburo, *KOGUN: The Japanese Army in the Pacific War* (Quantico, Va.: Marine Corps Association, 1959). The United States Strategic Bombing Survey also published a series of important studies and materials on the Pacific war. The developments which ended the fighting are still best covered in Robert J. C. Butow, *Japan's Decision to Surrender* (Stanford, Calif.: Stanford University Press, 1954).

The fighting between Japan and China awaits an English language history; readers will be greatly helped by F. F. Liu's *A Military History of Modern China, 1924-1949* (Princeton, N.J.: Princeton University Press, 1956), John H. Boyle, *China and Japan at War, 1937-1945: The Politics of Collaboration* (Stanford, Calif.: Stanford University Press, 1972), and Gerald E. Bunker, *The Peace Conspiracy: Wang Ching-wei and the China War, 1937-1941* (Cambridge, Mass.: Harvard University Press, 1972). The American role is covered in the three volumes by Charles Romanus and Riley Sutherland in the army's official history. The British fight for Burma is also dealt with in a multi-volume official history by C. Woodburn

Kirby, but it is more easily approached through Ronald Lewin's work on a key British commander, *Slim, The Standardbearer: A Biography of Field-Marshal The Viscount Slim* (London: Leo Cooper, 1976). The place of the Indian subcontinent in the war is surveyed by Johannes H. Voigt, *Indien im Zweiten Weltkrieg* (Stuttgart: Deutsche Verlags-Anstalt, 1978).

The brief listings provided here will be easily faulted by anyone familiar with even a small portion of the literature. The memoirs (except for Churchill's), collected papers, documentary publications, campaign and unit histories, as well as other whole bodies of literature have been omitted. No articles are listed at all, and many topics and areas have been left unmentioned. These omissions are neither judgments on the quality of the works left unmentioned nor assessments of the fields overlooked. The exclusions are arbitrary and designed to hold the quantity of books listed to a minimum. Those interested in additional works on subjects alluded to here or wishing to read further on topics not covered herein will find the bibliographic aids mentioned at the beginning of great—and continuing—help.

Index

All former colonial territories are referred to by their 1939 names.

Library of Congress Cataloging in Publication Data

Weinberg, Gerhard L.
World in the balance.

(The Tauber Institute series; no. 1)
Bibliography: p.
Includes index.
1. World War, 1939-1945—Germany—Addresses, essays, lectures. 2. Hitler, Adolf, 1889-1945—Addresses, essays, lectures. 3. Germany—History—1933-1945—Addresses, essays, lectures. I. Title. II. Series.
D757.W385 940.53'43 81-51606
ISBN 0-87451-216-6 AACR2
ISBN 0-87451-217-4 (pbk.)

Printed in the U
135651LV000

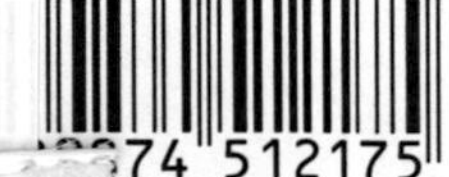